Grammar **joy** 2

저자 **이 종 저**

이화여자대학교 졸업
Longman Grammar Joy 1, 2, 3, 4권
Longman Vocabulary Mentor Joy 1, 2, 3권
I am Grammar 1, 2권
Grammar & Writing Level A 1, 2권 / Level B 1, 2권
Polybooks Grammar joy start 1, 2, 3, 4권
Polybooks Grammar joy 1, 2, 3, 4권
Polybooks 기본을 잡아주는 중등 영문법 1a,1b,2a,2b,3a,3b권
Polybooks 문법을 잡아주는 영작 1, 2, 3, 4권
Polybooks Grammar joy & Writing 1, 2, 3, 4권
Polybooks Bridging 초등 Voca 1, 2권
Polybooks Joy 초등 Voca 1, 2권

감수 **Jeanette Lee**

Wellesley college 졸업

지은이 | 이종저
펴낸곳 | POLY books
펴낸이 | POLY 영어 교재 연구소
기 획 | 박정원
편집디자인 | 이은경
삽화 | 이수진
초판 1쇄 인쇄 | 2015년 4월 25일
초판 21쇄 발행 | 2023년 2월 10일

POLY 영어 교재 연구소
경기도 성남시 분당구 황새울로 200번길 28 1128호
전화 070-7799-1583
ISBN | 979-11-86924-25-9
      979-11-86924-23-5(set)

Grammar joy 2

그 동안 Grammar Mentor Joy에 보내 주신 아낌없는 사랑과 관심에 힘입어 저자가 직접 Grammar Joy 시리즈의 개정판을 출간하게 되었습니다. 이에 더욱 학생들의 효과적인 학습에 도움이 될 수 있도록 연구개발하여 새롭게 선보이게 되었습니다.

영어 문법을 쉽고 재미있게 가르치고 배우길 바라며

본 개정판은 이전 학습자 및 선생님들의 의견과 영어 시장의 새로운 흐름에 맞춰 현장 교육을 바탕으로 집필하였습니다.

Grammar Joy는 다년간 현장 교육을 바탕으로, 학생의 눈높이와 학습 패턴에 맞춘 개념 설명, 재미있고 능동적이며 반복학습을 통해 자신도 모르는 사이에 영어 어휘와 문법을 익혀 나갈 수 있도록 합니다.

기본기를 확실히 다지도록 합니다

학생들은 대체로, 처음엔 영어에 흥미를 가지다가도 일정 시간이 흐르면 점차 어려워하고 지겹게 느끼기 시작합니다. 하지만, 기본 실력을 다지고 어느 정도 영어에 흥미를 계속 유지하도록 지도하면 어느 순간 실력이 월등해지고 재미를 붙여 적극성을 띠게 되는 것이 영어 학습입니다. Grammar Joy는 영어 학습에 꾸준히 흥미를 가질 수 있도록 기본기를 다져 줍니다.

어려운 정통 문법은 나중으로 미룹니다

영어에도 공식이 있습니다. 물론 실력자들은 공식이 아니라 어법이라고 하지요. 하지만 처음부터 어려운 어법을 강요하기보다는 쉬운 수학문제처럼, 어휘의 활용과 어순을 쉽게 이해할 수 있도록 규칙적인 해법을 공식화할 필요가 있습니다. 매우 단순해 보이지만 이를 반복 학습하다보면 어느새 공식의 개념을 깨닫게 되고 나중엔 그 공식에 얽매이지 않고 스스로 활용할 수 있게 됩니다. 이 책에서 쉬운 문제를 집중해서 푸는 것이 바로 그 공식을 소화해 가는 과정이라고 할 수 있습니다.

생동감있는 다양한 문장들로 이루어져 있습니다

실생활에서도 자주 쓰이는 문장들로 구성하여 현장 학습효과를 낼 수 있도록 하였습니다.

최고보다는 꼭 필요한 교재이고자 합니다

다년간 현장 교육을 통해, 학생들이 기존 문법 체계에 적응하기 어려워한다는 사실을 발견하였습니다. 학생들의 눈높이에 맞춰 흥미로운 학습 내용을 다루면서 자연스럽게 문법과 연계되는 내용들을 다루었습니다. 특히 이번 개정판은 기본을 잡아주는 중등영문법(Grammar Joy Plus)와 연계하여 중학교 내신에 대비에 부족함이 없도록 내용을 구성하였으므로 Grammar Joy를 끝내고 기본을 잡아주는 중등영문법(Grammar Joy Plus)를 공부한다면, 쓸데없는 중복 학습을 피하고 알찬 중학과정의 grammar 까지 완성할 수 있을 것이라 믿습니다.

모쪼록, 이 교재를 통해 선생님과 학생들이 재미있고 흥미있는 학습으로 소기의 성과를 얻을 수 있기를 기대하며 그동안 이번 시리즈를 출간하느라 함께 이해하며 동행해 주었던 이은경님께 아울러 감사드립니다.

저자 이종저

Contents

Unit 01 There is~, There are~ ·········· 12

Unit 02 일반동사의 긍정문 ················ 28

Unit 03 일반동사의 부정문과 의문문 ········ 48

Unit 04 현재진행형 ····················· 70

Review Test 1 ························· 90
내신대비 1 ····························· 98

Unit 05 형용사 ······················· 104

Unit 06 some, any와 many, much, a lot of ························· 128

Unit 07 부사 ·························· 146

Unit 08 비교 ·························· 166

Review Test 2 ······················· 184
내신대비 2 ···························· 192
종합문제 ····························· 198

Series Contents

Joy 1

Unit 01 셀 수 있는 명사
Unit 02 셀 수 없는 명사
Unit 03 관사
Unit 04 인칭대명사와 지시대명사
Unit 05 지시대명사와 지시형용사
Unit 06 인칭대명사의 격변화
Unit 07 be동사의 긍정문
Unit 08 be동사의 부정문, 의문문

Joy 3

Unit 01 「의문사 + 일반동사」 의문문
Unit 02 「의문사 + be동사」 의문문
Unit 03 의문대명사와 의문형용사
Unit 04 의문부사 (1)
Unit 05 의문부사 (2)
Unit 06 접속사와 명령문
Unit 07 조동사(can, must)
Unit 08 전치사

Joy 4

Unit 01 기수, 서수
Unit 02 비인칭주어
Unit 03 be동사, 일반동사 과거형의 긍정문
Unit 04 과거형의 부정문, 의문문
Unit 05 과거 진행형
Unit 06 미래형
Unit 07 감탄문
Unit 08 부정의문문, 부가의문문

Guide to This Book

1 Unit별 핵심정리

가장 기초적인 문법 사항과 핵심 포인트를 알기 쉽게 제시하여 주의 환기 및 개념 이해를 돕습니다.

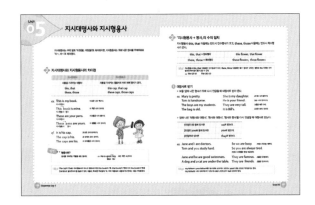

2 기초 다지기

Unit별 핵심 내용에 대한 매우 기초적인 확인 문제로, 개념 이해 및 스스로 문제를 풀어 보는 연습을 할 수 있도록 합니다.

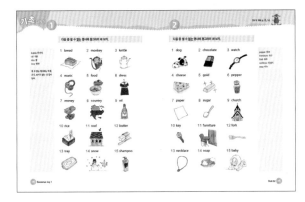

3 꼭꼭 다지기

기초 다지기보다 다소 난이도 있는 연습문제로, 앞서 배운 내용을 복습할 수 있도록 합니다.

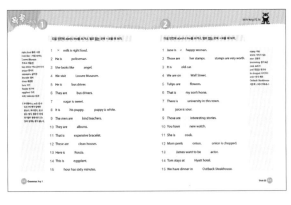

4 실력 다지기

다양한 형태로 제시되는 확장형 응용문제를 통해 문법 개념을 확실히 이해하고 실력을 굳힐 수 있도록 합니다.

5 실전 테스트

Unit별 마무리 테스트로서, 해당 Unit에서 배운 모든 문법 개념이 적용된 문제 풀이를 통해 응용력을 키우고 학교 선행학습에 대비할 수 있도록 합니다.

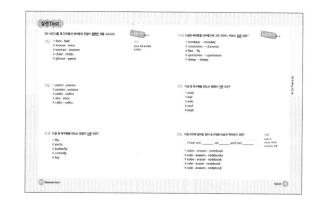

6 Quiz

한 Unit이 끝난 뒤에 쉬어가는 페이지로서, 앞서 배운 내용을 퀴즈 형태로 재미있게 풀어보고 다음 Unit로 넘어갈 수 있도록 합니다.

7 Review 테스트, 내신 대비

그 동안 배운 내용을 다시 한 번 복습할 수 있도록 이미 학습한 Unit에 대한 주관식 문제와 내신 대비를 위한 객관식 문제들을 풀어 보도록 합니다.

8 종합문제

최종 마무리 테스트로서, Unit 1~8 전체에 대한 종합적인 학습 내용을 다시 한번 점검하고 취약 부분을 파악할 수 있도록 합니다.

How to Use This Book

Grammar Joy Series는 전체 4권으로 구성되었으며, 각 권당 6주, 총 6개월의 수업 분량으로 기획되었습니다. 학습자와 학습 시간의 차이에 따라 문제 풀이 단계가운데 일부를 과제로 부여하거나 보충 수업을 통하여 시수를 맞출 수 있도록 하였습니다. 또한, 아래 제시된 진행 방식 외에, 학생들이 취약한 학습 영역을 다룬 교재를 먼저 채택하여 수업하실 수도 있습니다.

Month	Course	Week	Hour	Curriculum (Unit)	Homework/ Extra Curriculum
1st Month	Joy 1	1st	1	1. 셀 수 있는 명사	▶각 Unit별 퀴즈 ▶시수별 단어 풀이 과제 부여 또는 수업 중 단어 실력 테스트 ▶Review Test 내신대비
			2		
			3		
	Joy 1	2nd	1	2. 셀 수 없는 명사	
			2		
			3	3. 관사	
	Joy 1	3rd	1		
			2	4. 인칭대명사와 지시대명사	
			3		
	Joy 1	4th	1	5. 지시대명사와 지시형용사	
			2		
			3		
2nd Month	Joy 1	1st	1	6. 인칭대명사의 격변화	
			2		
			3	7. be동사의 긍정문	
	Joy 1	2nd	1		
			2	8. be동사의 부정문, 의문문	
			3		
	Joy 2	3rd	1	1. There is~/There are~	▶각 Unit별 퀴즈 ▶시수별 단어 풀이 과제 부여 또는 수업 중 단어 실력 테스트 ▶Review Test 내신대비
			2		
			3	2. 일반동사의 긍정문	
	Joy 2	4th	1		
			2	3. 일반동사의 부정문과 의문문	
			3		
3rd Month	Joy 2	1st	1	4. 현재진행형	
			2		
			3		
	Joy 2	2nd	1	5. 형용사	
			2		
			3		
	Joy 2	3rd	1	6. some, any와 many, much, a lot of	
			2		
			3	7. 부사	
	Joy 2	4th	1		
			2	8. 비교	
			3		

Month	Course	Week	Hour	Curriculum (Unit)	Homework/Extra Curriculum
4th Month	Joy 3	1st	1	**1.** 「의문사 + 일반동사」 의문문	▶ 각 Unit별 퀴즈 ▶ 시수별 단어 풀이 과제 부여 또는 수업 중 단어 실력 테스트 ▶ Review Test 내신대비
			2		
			3		
	Joy 3	2nd	1	**2.** 「의문사 + be동사」 의문문	
			2		
			3	**3.** 의문대명사와 의문형용사	
	Joy 3	3rd	1		
			2	**4.** 의문부사(1)	
			3		
	Joy 3	4th	1	**5.** 의문부사(2)	
			2		
			3	**6.** 접속사와 명령문	
5th Month	Joy 3	1st	1		
			2	**7.** 조동사(can, must)	
			3		
	Joy 3	2nd	1	**8.** 전치사	
			2		
			3		
	Joy 4	3rd	1	**1.** 기수, 서수	▶ 각 Unit별 퀴즈 ▶ 시수별 단어 풀이 과제 부여 또는 수업 중 단어 실력 테스트 ▶ Review Test 내신대비 ▶ 종합문제
			2		
			3	**2.** 비인칭주어	
	Joy 4	4th	1		
			2	**3.** be동사, 일반동사 과거형의 긍정문	
			3		
6th Month	Joy 4	1st	1		
			2		
			3	**4.** 과거형의 부정문, 의문문	
	Joy 4	2nd	1		
			2	**5.** 과거진행형	
			3		
	Joy 4	3rd	1	**6.** 미래형	
			2		
			3	**7.** 감탄문	
	Joy 4	4th	1	**8.** 부정의문문, 부가의문문	
			2		
			3		

No pains, no gains.

Unit 01

There is~,
There are~

There is~, There are~ 구문에서는
be동사가 「~이 있다」라는 뜻으로 쓰인다.
There는 '거기에'라는 뜻이 있지만,
이 경우에는 해석하지 않는다.

There is~, There are~

두 가지 의미를 갖는 be동사(am, are, is)

❶ ~이다 : 주어의 상태를 표현할 때

　　ex. She is my friend. 　그녀는 나의 친구이다.

❷ ~(이) 있다 : 장소나 위치를 나타내는 말과 함께 올 때

　　ex. She is in the classroom. 　그녀는 교실에 있다.

1 There is, There are~

① There is~, There are~ 구문에서는 be동사가 「~이 있다」라는 뜻으로 쓰인다.
There는 '거기에' 라는 뜻이 있지만, 단순히 문장을 유도하기 위한 부사이므로,
이 경우에는 해석하지 않는다.

　ex. **There is** a book on the desk. 　책상 위에 책이 한 권 있다.

② 위 문장에서는 주어가 there가 아니고 a book이다. There is~,
There are~에서는 주어가 문장의 맨 앞이 아닌 be동사(is) 바로 뒤에 위치하고 있음에 유의한다.

2 긍정문

There is 다음에는 단수 명사나 셀 수 없는 명사가 오고, There are 다음에는 복수 명사가 온다.

There is	+ 단수 명사, 셀 수 없는 명사	~이 있다
There are	+ 복수 명사	~들이 있다.

　ex. **There is an orange** on the table. 　　탁자 위에 오렌지가 하나 있다.
　　　 There is some juice in the glass. 　　유리잔에 약간의 주스가 있다.

　ex. **There are two oranges** on the table. 　탁자 위에 두 개의 오렌지가 있다.
　　　 ~~There is two oranges on the table.~~

> **Tip!** something, anything, nothing은 단수로 취급하여 there is로 쓴다.
> 　*ex.* There is something in it. 그것 안에 무언가가 있다.

부정문

be동사 뒤에 **not**을 붙이면 「～이 없다, ～이 있지 않다」의 뜻이 된다.

There is	+not	~.
There are		

ex. **There is not** a ball in the box. 　　　　　상자 안에 공이 없다.

　　There are not a lot of balls in the box. 　상자 안에 공들이 많이 없다.

 의문문

be동사를 there 앞으로 보내고 문장 끝에 물음표를 붙이면 '～이 있니?'라고 묻는 말이 된다.

Is	there	~?
Are		

ex. **Is there** a ball in the box? 　　　　　　상자 안에 공이 있니?

　Are there a lot of balls in the box? 　상자 안에 많은 공들이 있니?

대답은 Yes, there is. No, there isn't. Yes, there are. No, there aren't. 로 하면 된다.

Is there a ball in the box?　　　　　　- Yes, **there is.** 　　　네, 그래요.

　　　　　　　　　　　　　　　　　　　　- No, **there isn't.** 　아니오, 그렇지 않아요.

Are there many balls in the box?　　　- Yes, **there are.** 　　네, 그래요.

　　　　　　　　　　　　　　　　　　　　- No, **there aren't.** 아니오, 그렇지 않아요.

 be동사는 「～이 있다」라는 뜻을 가지고 있으므로 There is/are~는 ~is/are로 바꿔 쓸 수 있다.

ex. **There is** a cap on the bed.

　　= A cap **is** on the bed. 　침대 위에 모자가 있다.

> **Tip!** There is/are 뒤에는 특정한 명사가 올 수 없다.
> *ex.* ~~There is **the** bank in the city.~~ 　　　　　~~There is **his** bag on the bench.~~
> 　　The bank is in the city. 그 은행은 그 도시에 있다. 　His bag is on the bench. 그의 가방은 벤치 위에 있다.

다음 ( ) 안에서 알맞은 동사를 골라 동그라미 해 보자.

dolphin 돌고래
aquarium 수족관
player 선수
soccer team 축구팀
center 중앙
a lot of 많은 = much,
many
traffic light 신호등
among ~가운데
little ~ 거의 없는
a little 약간의
refrigerator 냉장고
something 어떤 것, 무엇
beside ~옆에
in front of ~앞에

12 something,
anything,
nothing은
there is로 받는다.

1 There (is, are) a dolphin in the aquarium.

2 There (is, are) 26 players in this soccer team.

3 There (is, are) a picture in the center.

4 There (is, are) some milk in the bottle.

5 There (is, are) three glasses of milk on the table.

6 There (is, are) a lot of traffic lights on this road.

7 There (is, are) a handsome boy among the girls.

8 There (is, are) little soup in the bowl.

9 There (is, are) twenty tables in the restaurant.

10 There (is, are) a little food in the refrigerator.

11 There (is, are) 852 students in our school.

12 There (is, are) something over there.

13 There (is, are) an eraser under the desk.

14 There (is, are) some forks beside a knife.

15 There (is, are) two children in front of the bus.

2

다음 빈칸에 is와 are 중에서 알맞은 말을 골라 써 보자.

1 There *is* a kitten behind the curtain.

2 There _____ a few pickles in the jar.

3 There _____ five coins in his pocket.

4 There _____ some dogs in the pet shop.

5 There _____ a hotel far from here.

6 There _____ a cell phone in his car.

7 There _____ four loaves of bread by the basket.

8 There _____ some boys at the taxi stand.

9 There _____ Sumi and Jane behind the tree.

10 There _____ nothing for you.

11 There _____ six rooms in the house.

12 There _____ a train at 10 p.m.

13 There _____ a mosquito in the room.

14 There _____ ten waiters in the restaurant.

15 There _____ a snake on the grass.

kitten 새끼고양이
curtain 커튼
a few 약간의
pet shop 애완 동물 가게
taxi stand 택시 정류장
behind ~뒤에
nothing 아무것
mosquito 모기
waiter 웨이터
grass 잔디

우리말에 알맞게 빈칸을 채워 보자.

hairdresser 미용사
beauty shop 미용실
a film festival 영화제
salt 소금
pillow 베개
subway station 지하철역
convenience store 편의점
mountain 산
something 무엇인가

1   *There   are   three pencils*   in the pencil case.
필통 안에 연필 세 자루가 있다.

2   in the beauty salon.
미용실에 다섯 명의 미용사가 있다.

3   next month.
다음 달에 영화제가 있다.

4   in this soup.
이 수프에는 많은 소금이 들어 있다.

5   on his bed.
그의 침대위에 두 개의 베게가 있다.

6   in the pot.
주전자 안에 약간의 차가 있다.

7   at the subway station.
지하철역에 많은 사람들이 있다.

8   across the street.
길 건너에 편의점이 있다.

9   behind our house.
우리 집 뒤에 산이 있다.

10. something,
anything, nothing은
there is로 받는다.

10   in my eyes.
내 눈에 무엇인가가 있다.

4

다음 문장을 지시대로 바꾸고, 의문문은 대답도 완성해 보자.

1 There are two candies by the box.

의문문 _Are_ _there_ two candies by the box?

– Yes, _there_ _are_ .

2 There is an American teacher in my school.

의문문 an American teacher in my school?

– No, .

3 There are three hairpins in her hand.

부정문 three hairpins in her hand.

4 There is a lot of money in her purse.

의문문 a lot of money in her purse?

– Yes, .

5 There are 20 doctors in this hospital.

의문문 20 doctors in this hospital?

– No, .

6 There is a book between the pen and the ruler.

의문문 a book between the pen and the

ruler?

– Yes, .

7 There are a lot of students in the school library.

부정문 many students in the school library.

8 There is a big difference between the two.

부정문 a big difference between the two.

by~ ~옆에
in her hand 그녀의 손에
purse (어깨끈이 없는)
핸드백
cf. wallet (남성용) 지갑
school library
학교 도서관
between A and B
A와 B 사이
difference 차이

4. money는 셀 수 없는
명사이다.

다음 우리말에 알맞게 빈칸을 채워 보자.

second 초
minute 분
amusement park 놀이공원
outside 밖에
under ~밑에
present 선물
plastic bag 비닐봉지

1 *There* *are* four people in my family.
나의 가족은 네 명의 사람이 있다.

2 _____ sixty seconds in a minute.
1분에는 60초가 있다.

3 _____ a lot of churches in Seoul.
서울에는 많은 교회가 없다.

4 _____ a coffee shop in this buliding.
이 건물에는 커피숍이 없다.

5 _____ a zoo in the amusement park.
그 놀이공원에는 동물원이 없다.

6 _____ a cat outside your house.
너의 집 밖에 고양이가 있다.

7 _____ a blue jacket under the bench.
벤치 아래 파란 자켓이 없다.

8 _____ cookies in the plastic bag.
비닐봉지 안에 과자들이 없다.

9 _____ anything in my pocket.
나의 주머니에 어떤 것도 없다.

10 _____ two melons in the refrigerator.
냉장고에 두 개의 멜론이 있다.

2

다음 문장을 뜻이 같은 문장으로 바꿔 써 보자.

1 There are some tennis balls on this tennis court.

= _Some tennis balls_ _are_ on this tennis court.

2 A university is in this city.

= in this city.

3 There are five events every year.

= every year.

4 A jumper is in Tom's closet.

= in Tom's closet.

5 A lot of rice is in the rice cooker.

= in the rice cooker.

6 There are five oceans in the world.

= in the world.

7 There is some food in the house.

= in the house.

8 Seven Italian restaurants are in this town.

= in this town.

9 A man is at the end of the street.

= at the end of the street.

10 There is a free coupon in her purse.

= in her purse.

tennis court 테니스 코트
university 대학
event 사건
year 해, 년
jumper 점퍼
closet 옷장
rice cooker 밥솥
ocean 큰 바다, 태양
world 세계
refrigerator 냉장고
Italian 이탈리아의,
이탈리아 사람
town 마을
free coupon 무료쿠폰
purse 여성용 지갑

다음 밑줄 친 부분들 중에서 **틀린** 곳을 바르게 고쳐 써 보자.

parking lot 주차장
grape 포도
museum 박물관
hour 시간
teddy bear 테디 베어, 봉제
곰인형
trash 쓰레기
special 특별한
mailbox 우편함
post office 우체국
cutting board 도마

6. some + 셀 수 없는 명사
→ 단수 취급

12. nothing은 단수 취급
한다.

1 There <u>is</u> some <u>bananas</u> on the table.
　　　are

2 There <u>are</u> a <u>carton</u> of juice in the refrigerator.

3 There <u>is</u> two <u>students</u> in the gym.

4 Many cars <u>isn't</u> in the parking lot.

5 Three <u>bunches</u> of grapes <u>is</u> in the box.

6 <u>Some</u> cheese <u>are</u> on the dish.

7 Two <u>pieces</u> of cheese <u>is</u> on the dish.

8 Ten old <u>man</u> <u>aren't</u> in the museum.

9 There <u>are</u> 24 <u>hour</u> in a day.

10 There <u>is</u> two teddy <u>bears</u> on the sofa.

11 There <u>are</u> a lot of <u>trash</u> on the street.

12 <u>There</u> <u>are</u> nothing special.

13 There <u>is</u> <u>few</u> letters in the mailbox.

14 There <u>aren't</u> a few <u>peoples</u> in the post office.

15 A cutting <u>boards</u> <u>is</u> in the kitchen.

2

다음 밑줄 친 부분들 중에서 **틀린** 곳을 바르게 고쳐 써 보자.

1 There <u>is</u> 10 <u>belts</u> in the clothing store.
   are

2 A lot of <u>crab</u> <u>are</u> on the beach.

3 Four <u>lions</u> <u>is</u> in the field.

4 There <u>is</u> 60 <u>minutes</u> in an hour.

5 There <u>are</u> some <u>paper</u> on the desk.

6 There <u>are</u> <u>a lot of</u> snow in winter.

7 Some <u>dancer</u> <u>are</u> on the stage.

8 There <u>are</u> a comb on <u>the table</u>.

9 There <u>is</u> a lot of <u>computers</u> in his office.

10 There <u>are</u> <u>something</u> chic about Tom.

11 A kitten <u>are</u> under the <u>chair</u>.

12 <u>There</u> <u>is</u> five bunches of grapes in the box.

13 101 <u>dog</u> <u>are</u> in the house.

14 There <u>are</u> five English <u>class</u> in a week.

15 There <u>is</u> two <u>pieces</u> of furniture in the hall.

clothing store 옷 가게
crab 게
beach 해변
field 들판
stage 무대
office 사무실
chic 멋진, 세련된
kitten 새끼 고양이
furniture 가구

01 다음 빈칸에 들어갈 말로 알맞은 것은?

> There is _____ on the desk.

① a lot of books
② a computer
③ an eraser and a ruler
④ some apples
⑤ a few pencils

02 다음 대화의 빈칸에 들어갈 말로 알맞은 것은?

> A : Are there any dolls on the piano?
>
> B : _____

① Yes, they are.
② No, they aren't.
③ Yes, there is.
④ There aren't.
⑤ Yes, there are.

03 다음 빈칸에 들어갈 말로 알맞은 것은?

| There _____ some water in the bottle. |

① am   ② are
③ is   ④ have
⑤ has

03

water는 셀 수 없는 명사
이다.

04 다음 두 문장이 같은 뜻이 되도록 할 때, 빈칸에 들어갈 말로 알맞은 것은?

| There are three cats in the box. |
| = Three cats _____ in the box. |

① is   ② are
③ has   ④ have
⑤ do

05 다음 밑줄 친 is의 뜻이 <u>다른</u> 것은?

① Some sugar <u>is</u> in the bottle.
② Jack <u>is</u> in front of his house.
③ This <u>is</u> a very interesting story.
④ A banana <u>is</u> on the table.
⑤ Mr. Kim <u>is</u> in the museum.

06 다음 질문에 대한 대답으로 알맞은 것은?

> Is there a big tree in this park?

① Yes, it is.
② No, it isn't.
③ Yes, they are.
④ No, there isn't.
⑤ No, there aren't.

07 다음 문장에서 <u>틀린</u> 곳을 바르게 고쳐 쓰시오.

> There are a museum in this town.

_____ ⇨ _____

07
There 뒤의 be동사는
주어에 따라 달라진다.

08 다음 문장을 부정문으로 바꿔 쓰시오.

> There is a baby by the sofa.
>
> → _____

09 다음 (A), (B)의 빈칸에 들어갈 말을 |보기|에서 고를 때, 바르게 짝지어진 것은?

| 보기 | ⓐ two pieces of cake

  ⓑ some soup

(A) There is _____ on the dish.

(B) There are _____ in the bowl.

① (A) – ⓐ, (B) – ⓑ   ② (A) – ⓑ, (B) – ⓐ

③ (A) – ⓐ, (B) – ⓐ   ④ (A) – ⓑ, (B) – ⓑ

⑤ 모두 틀림

10 다음 우리말에 맞도록 (   ) 안의 단어를 배열하여 문장을 쓰시오.

나비 세 마리가 정원에 있니?

(three, in, are, the, butterflies, there, garden, ?)

⇨ _____

10
butterfly 나비
garden 정원

주어진 단어를 이용해 우리말에 알맞게 빈칸을 채워 보자.

1 _____ in the pond. (water)

연못에 많은 물이 있다.

2 _____ on the wall. (map)

벽에 지도가 없다.

3 _____ in a year. (month)

일 년에 12달이 있다.

4 _____ in the oven. (bread)

오븐 안에 약간의 빵이 있다.

5 _____ on the ceiling. (spider)

천장에 거미가 없다.

6 _____ on the road. (snow)

길 위에 많은 눈이 있다.

7 _____ in September. (Sunday)

9월에는 4개의 일요일이 있다.

8 _____ in her cup. (coffee)

그녀의 컵에 약간의 커피가 있다.

9 _____ in the plastic bag. (flour)

비닐 봉투 안에 많은 밀가루가 있다.

10 _____ by the sofa. (dog)

소파 옆에 개가 없다.

Unit 02

일반동사의 긍정문

be동사와 조동사를 제외한
나머지 동사를 일반동사라고 하며,
주어의 동작이나 상태를 나타낸다.

일반동사의 긍정문

일반동사란?

be동사(am, are, is)와 조동사(can, will, must…)를 제외한 나머지 동사를 말하며, 주어의 동작이나 상태를 나타낸다.

1 주어+ 일반동사

일반동사는 현재 시제일 때 주어에 따라 형태가 변한다. 주어가 3인칭 단수일 때 「동사원형 + s, es」의 형태를 쓰고, 나머지는 모두 동사원형을 그대로 쓴다.

단수		복수	
I	동사원형 ~.	We	동사원형 ~.
You		You	
He	동사원형 + s, es ~.	They	
She			
It			

ex. I like it.　　　　We like it.
　　You (너는) like it.　　You (너희들은) like it.
　　He like**s** it.　　　They like it.
　　She like**s** it.
　　Tom like**s** it.

잠깐　● **동사원형이란?**
우리말에서 '간다. 갈 것이다. 갔다…'등이 모두 '가다'에서 변화된 것처럼 영어에서도 'goes, going, went…' 등은 모두 go가 변형된 것이다. 이렇게 go처럼 뿌리가 되는 형태를 동사의 원형이라고 한다.

일반동사의 3인칭 단수형

주어가 3인칭 단수이고, 시제가 현재일 때 다음과 같이 일반동사에 s, es를 붙여 3인칭 단수형으로 만든다.

종류	공식		예
규칙 변화	대부분의 동사	+ s	run → runs
	e로 끝나는 동사	+ s	love → loves like → likes
	모음 + y로 끝나는 동사	+ s	enjoy → enjoys pay → pays play → plays
	자음 + y로 끝나는 동사	y → ies	cry → cries study → studies try → tries
	ch, sh, s, x로 끝나는 동사	+ es	fix → fixes pass → passes wash → washes watch → watches
불규칙 변화	무조건 외운다		do → does go → goes have → has

enjoy 즐기다
pay 지불하다
cry 울다
try 시도하다
fix 수리하다
pass 통과하다
wash 씻다
watch 보다
do 하다

Tip! 규칙적인 변화를 하는 명사의 복수형의 공식과 유사하다.

ex. The baby cries at night.   그 아기는 밤에 운다.
   The babies cry at night.   그 아기들은 밤에 운다.

ex. The policeman catches the robber.   그 경찰관은 강도를 잡는다.
   The policemen catch the robber.   그 경찰관들은 강도를 잡는다.

ex. Tom goes to school.   Tom은 학교에 다닌다.
   Tom and Mary go to school.   Tom과 Mary는 학교에 다닌다.

주어가 3인칭 단수일 때 동사의 형태이다. 알맞은 것을 골라 보자.

catch 잡다
reply 대답하다
coach 코치하다
pray 기도하다
touch 만지다
miss 놓치다, 그리워하다
pitch 던지다

1 push (pushs, pushes)   **2** like (likes, liks)

3 sit (sits, sites)   **4** catch (catchs, catches)

5 pass (passs, passes)   **6** hold (holdes, holds)

7 wash (washes, washs)   **8** try (trys, tries)

9 reply (replies, replys)   **10** work (works, workes)

11 say (saies, says)   **12** ask (asks, askes)

13 take (takes, takees)   **14** send (sends, sendes)

15 wax (waxs, waxes)   **16** coach (coachs, coaches)

17 cry (crys, cries)   **18** come (comes, coms)

19 miss (misses, missies)   **20** read (reads, reades)

21 do (dos, does)   **22** pray (praies, prays)

23 play (plaies, plays)   **24** teach (teachs, teaches)

25 touch (touchs, touches)   **26** tell (telles, tells)

27 mix (mixes, mixs)   **28** wax (waxs, waxes)

29 see (sees, seeies)   **30** pitch (pitches, pitchs)

주어가 3인칭 단수일 때 동사의 형태를 써 보자.

1 meet	*meets*	**2** walk	
3 fly		**4** hit	
5 finish		**6** love	
7 pass		**8** hear	
9 have		**10** toss	
11 solve		**12** play	
13 fry		**14** match	
15 guess		**16** eat	
17 watch		**18** write	
19 fix		**20** draw	
21 begin		**22** push	
23 go		**24** enjoy	
25 pay		**26** hate	
27 study		**28** stay	
29 kiss		**30** live	

toss (공을) 튀기다
solve 풀다
match 어울리다
guess 추측하다
push 밀다

다음 (   ) 안에서 알맞은 동사의 형태를 골라 동그라미 해 보자.

toy 장난감
do one's best 최선을 다하다
science 과학
garden 정원
newspaper 신문
earth 지구
move 움직이다
grow 재배하다
take care of ~을 돌보다
bird 새

1   I (have, has) a toy.

2   He (do, does) his best.

3   They (study, studies) science.

4   Mary and Jane (go, goes) to bed before 9.

5   She (learn, learns) English.

6   The house (have, has) a large garden.

7   Matt (bring, brings) a newspaper.

8   The students (open, opens) their books.

9   The earth (move, moves) around the sun.

10   The new cell phone (catch, catches) my eyes.

11   She (grow, grows) a lot of tomatoes.

12   You (close, closes) the door.

13   The child (like, likes) sweet candies.

14   He (take, takes) care of the baby.

15   We (visit, visits) some poor people.

4

다음 ( ) 안에서 알맞은 동사의 형태를 골라 동그라미 해 보자.

1 He (toss, tosses) me.

2 My brothers (push, pushes) the car.

3 Mrs. Brown (teach, teaches) art.

4 Sumi and I (finish, finishes) the work.

5 Maria and Jim (do, does) their homework.

6 Her boyfriend (give, gives) her one hundred roses.

7 The girls (listen, listens) to classical music.

8 It (take, takes) 10 minutes.

9 She (live, lives) in an apartment.

10 We (clean, cleans) up the gym.

11 My mother (eat, eats) some cucumbers.

12 The painter (live, lives) in France.

13 She (want, wants) to marry Tom.

14 They (hear, hears) the strange sound.

15 He (look, looks) like a singer.

teach 가르치다
art 미술
hundred 백 개의
classical music 클래식 음악
listen to ~을 듣다
take (시간이) 걸리다
apartment 아파트
cucumber 오이
painter 화가
France 프랑스
marry 결혼하다
strange 이상한
sound 소리
look like ~처럼 보이다
singer 가수

다음 ( ) 안에 알맞은 말을 골라 동그라미 해 보자.

apple pie 사과 파이
stay 머무르다
respect 존경하다
wait for ~를 기다리다
turn 돌다
right 오른쪽
win 이기다
movie 영화
aunt 아주머니, 고모, 이모
fresh 신선한
air 공기
uncle 아저씨
forget 잊다
hunt 사냥하다
work (계획 등이) 잘 되다
try to ~하려고 시도하다
put on ~을 입다

1 (You, My mom, We) makes an apple pie.

2 (He, Tom, We) stay in Seoul.

3 (We, You, She) comes home early.

4 (She, The boy, They) respect him.

5 (I, You, Paul) sees many people at the bus stop.

6 (You, Tom and Mary, John) waits for us.

7 (He, We, He and she) turns to the right.

8 (Inho, Her brother, We) win the game.

9 (Mary, Jane and Judy) watch a movie.

10 (She, He, We) need fresh air.

11 (My aunt, My uncles, I) forgets it.

12 (The lions, The tiger) hunts a deer.

13 (They, It) works well.

14 (You, Julie's friend) try to put on the shirt.

15 (He, She, He and she) swim in the river.

6

다음 ( ) 안에 알맞은 말을 골라 동그라미 해 보자.

1 (Jim, Ann and Jim) coaches football team.

2 (My friend, My friends) says hello to her.

3 (Mary and Joe, He, Sam) enter the hospital.

4 (He and she, He) resembles his father.

5 (Tom, Judy, I) slip and fall down.

6 (The scientist, The scientists) believe that.

7 (They, The girl, He) understand Mr. Smith.

8 (He, They, You) hurries up in the morning.

9 (He, You, She) look tired.

10 (The man, The men) shows me a map.

11 (She, You, They) brings two melons to me.

12 (A day, Days) has twenty-four hours.

13 (She, The children) cry all day long.

14 (The couples, He, She) carry their baggage.

15 (I, They, Mike) wears a pair of glasses.

say hello 안부를 전하다
enter 들어가다
resemble 닮다
slip 미끄러지다
fall down 넘어지다
scientist 과학자
believe 믿다, 신뢰하다
hurry 서두르다
look ~하게 보이다
tired 피곤한
bring 가지고 오다
all day long 하루 종일
baggage 짐, 수하물

14. couple은 복수 취급한다.

다음 (   ) 안의 동사를 현재형으로 바꿔 빈칸에 써 보자.

lose 잃어버리다
wallet (남성용) 지갑
arrive 도착하다
feel 느끼다
hill 꼭대기, 언덕
arrive 도착하다
blond hair 금발머리
wax 광을 내다

1 My daddy   *reads*   a novel. (read)

2 He   his wallet. (lose)

3 She   her report to me. (send)

4 Her brothers   Mr. Park. (remember)

5 Some bees   among the flowers. (fly)

6 Jane   her hands. (wash)

7 Mary and I   the woman. (know)

8 My grandparents   their plan. (change)

9 The gentleman   to her. (speak)

10 The child   so good. (feel)

11 Matt   his neck. (touch)

12 They   at school at 8. (arrive)

13 You   some meat. (buy)

14 The girls   beautiful blond hair. (have)

15 Cathy   her shoes. (wax)

2

다음 ( ) 안의 동사를 현재형으로 바꿔 빈칸에 써 보자.

1 My sisters *go* to church on Sundays. (go)

2 Harry a sandwich with ham. (make)

3 She the dishes. (do)

4 I for Italy. (leave)

5 Mrs. Baker it again. (try)

6 You and your mother to God. (pray)

7 Her necklace her dress. (match)

8 Jane up. (hurry)

9 You a car carefully. (drive)

10 Paul exams. (hate)

11 We some bread to them. (give)

12 The students attention to the teacher. (pay)

13 Mary her hair. (dry)

14 He a tennis racket. (get)

15 The young men life. (enjoy)

leave for ~향해 떠나다
Italy 이탈리아
try 시도하다
pray 기도하다
sometimes 가끔
carefully 조심스럽게
hate (몹시) 싫어하다
present 선물
pay attention to ~에게
주목하다
tennis racket 테니스 라켓
life 인생, 삶

다음 ( ) 안의 동사를 현재형으로 바꿔 빈칸에 써 보자.

carry 운반하다
hope 바라다, 희망하다
sound ~처럼 들리다
watermelon 수박
boss 상사
view 경치

1 He *carries* this sofa. (carry)

2 They _____ to have a new house. (hope)

3 It _____ good. (sound)

4 My father _____ to me. (say)

5 The girl _____ a taxi. (catch)

6 She _____ Jimmy. (kiss)

7 You _____ two watermelons. (have)

8 The old men _____ dinner. (eat)

9 Bill _____ a red pen (have)

10 I _____ the box. (pull)

11 The girl _____ a beautiful song. (sing)

12 My boss _____ in Europe. (travel)

13 Julia _____ her homework after school. (do)

14 My parents _____ at the view. (look)

15 She _____ it twice. (fry)

4

다음 ( ) 안의 동사를 현재형으로 바꿔 빈칸에 써 보자.

1 I _spend_ a lot of money. (spend)

2 Mary ___ about it. (think)

3 He ___ the job. (finish)

4 Her son ___ money back. (pay)

5 You ___ the laundry. (do)

6 The horse ___ a sweet potato. (bite)

7 The boy ___ a diary. (keep)

8 She ___ no classes on Friday. (have)

9 The students ___ here everyday. (study)

10 Mom ___ an egg and some flour. (mix)

11 Paul ___ his father. (miss)

12 They ___ on the subway. (get)

13 It ___ . (rain)

14 We ___ a trip. (take)

15 The mouse ___ to eat this cheese. (try)

spend 소비하다
pay ~ back 돌려주다
do the laundry 빨래하다
bite 깨물다
sweet potato 고구마
keep a diary 일기를 쓰다
class 수업
mix 섞다
flour 밀가루
miss 놓치다, 그리워하다
get on 타다
take a trip 여행하다

다음 밑줄 친 부분들 중에서 틀린 곳을 바르게 고쳐 써 보자.

take a nap 낮잠을 자다
at noon 정오에
for a living 생계를 위해
call out for help 도움을 구하다
crosswalk 횡단보도
nicely 멋지게
pass 건네주다, 통과하다
hug 껴안다
repeat 반복하다
sentence 문장

1 He take a nap at noon.
    takes

2 The man do it for a living.

3 The boys calls out for help.

4 She close her mouth.

5 His son cross the street in the crosswalk.

6 Your aunt drys your shirt.

7 We jumps nicely.

8 The movie end at 10.

9 Sue trys to make a kite.

10 The concert begin at 6.

11 My father fixs his car.

12 He pass me the salt.

13 The kid like to play with a dog.

14 The children hugs each other.

15 Tom and Ann repeats the sentences.

2

다음 밑줄 친 부분들 중에서 틀린 곳을 바르게 고쳐 써 보자.

1 The <u>boys</u> knows <u>them</u>.
   boy

2 The boy <u>pay</u> for school <u>supplies</u>.

3 She <u>wear</u> <u>a blue hat</u>.

4 Mr. Kim <u>haves</u> two <u>sons</u>.

5 <u>The girls</u> eats <u>something</u> all day.

6 The old <u>tigers</u> dies <u>alone</u> in the field.

7 The stars <u>shines</u> <u>in the sky</u>.

8 We <u>cooks</u> it <u>with</u> the recipe.

9 Judy <u>take</u> <u>a picture</u>.

10 The <u>baby</u> kiss the <u>doll</u>.

11 He <u>catchs</u> seven <u>mosquitoes</u>.

12 Mary and John <u>wants</u> to be a <u>scientist</u>.

13 My parents <u>sells</u> a lot of <u>rice</u>.

14 A student <u>replys</u> to <u>his</u> question.

15 The teacher <u>erase</u> the words <u>on the blackboard</u>.

school supplies 학용품
recipe 조리법
shine 빛나다
catch 잡다
erase 지우다
blackboard 칠판

실전Test

01 다음 중 동사원형과 3인칭 단수 현재형이 바르게 짝지어지지 <u>않은</u> 것은?

① swim - swims   ② run - runs

③ catch - catches   ④ marry - marrys

⑤ go - goes

02 다음 두 동사의 3인칭 단수 현재형이 바르게 짝지어진 것은?

fix   drive

① fixes - drivees   ② fixs - drives

③ fixes - drives   ④ fixes - drivs

⑤ fixs - drivs

03 다음 빈칸에 들어갈 말로 알맞은 것은?

_____ sleep well every day.

① You   ② He

③ My child   ④ She

⑤ Paul

04 다음 중 밑줄 친 부분이 바르지 <u>않은</u> 것은?

① She <u>pushs</u> the door.
② Tom <u>walks</u> to school.
③ Mary <u>loves</u> her father.
④ My mother <u>tries</u> to make a cake.
⑤ He <u>speaks</u> English very well.

05 다음 밑줄 친 동사를 올바른 형태로 고칠 때, 알맞은 것끼리 짝지어진 것은?

> · My brother <u>buy</u> a game CD.
>
> · Mary and John <u>know</u> us.

① buys - know
② buys - knows
③ buies - know
④ buy - know
⑤ buies - knows

실전Test

더알아보기

06 다음 (   ) 안의 동사를 현재형으로 바꿔 쓰시오.

(1) My parents _____ shopping. (go)
(2) He _____ me the picture. (show)
(3) John _____ tennis. (play)
(4) We _____ dinner at 7. (have)
(5) The girl _____ a song. (sing)

07 다음 빈칸에 들어갈 말로 알맞지 <u>않은</u> 것은?

> He _____ his robot.

① loves   ② sells
③ makes   ④ has
⑤ break

07

주어 He는 3인칭 단수
이다.

08 다음 동사들을 3인칭 단수 현재형으로 만들 때, 형태가 <u>다른</u> 하나는?

① study   ② try
③ carry   ④ play
⑤ worry

08

worry 근심하다

09 다음 우리말과 같은 뜻이 되도록 빈칸에 알맞은 말을 쓰시오.

> 나의 여동생은 피자를 좋아한다.
>
> → My sister _____ pizza.

09

My sister 는 3인칭 단수이다.

10 다음 빈칸에 들어갈 말로 알맞은 것은?

> _____ helps others. others 다른 사람들

① We
② They
③ The boys
④ You
⑤ Judy

10

동사 helps의 형태에 유의하여 주어를 찾는다.

정답 및 해설 **p.4**

Quiz!

1 (You, She, He) look after a little bird.

2 (They, She, The boy) show me their paintings.

3 (We, The businessmen, He) has a lot of money.

4 (His brothers, Her sister) passes the exam.

5 (The student, We, Ann) walk to the museum.

6 (These men, This man) touches the painting.

7 (Ann, I, Students) studies very hard.

다음 ( ) 안에 주어진 동사를 현재형으로 바꿔 보자.

1 He   his son. (love)

2 The girls   on the playground. (play)

3 She   breakfast at 7. (have)

4 The lady   a newspaper. (read)

5 They   their homework. (finish)

6 Mr. and Mrs. Brown   a rest. (take)

7 Tom   his computer. (sell)

8 My mother   shopping for the party. (go)

Unit o**3**

일반동사의
부정문과 의문문

일반동사의 부정문을 만들 때에는
일반동사 바로 앞에 don't를 쓰고,
주어가 3인칭 단수이면 doesn't를 쓴다.
일반동사의 의문문을 만들 때에는
Do나 Does를 쓴다.

일반동사의 부정문과 의문문

Unit 03

① 부정문

주어 + don't, doesn't + 동사원형

주어가 1, 2인칭 단/복수, 3인칭 복수인 경우에 일반동사 바로 앞에 **don't** (= do not)를 붙여 부정문을 만들고, 주어가 3인칭 단수일 경우에는 일반동사 바로 앞에 **doesn't** (= does not)를 붙여 부정문을 만든다. 이때, 일반동사는 **s**나 **es**가 붙지 않은 동사 원형이 온다.

단수		복수	
I	don't + 동사원형	We	don't + 동사원형
You		You	
He	doesn't + 동사원형	They	
She			
It			

ex. I **don't** like an apple.
You (너는) **don't** like an apple.
He **doesn't** likeₓ an apple.
She **doesn't** likeₓ an apple.
It **doesn't** likeₓ an apple.

We **don't** like an apple.
You (너희들은) **don't** like an apple.
They **don't** like an apple.

① too와 either

역시, ～도 또한

too	긍정문
either	부정문

ex. A : I like the singer. 나는 그 가수를 좋아해.
B : I **like** the singer, **too**. 나도 역시 그 가수를 좋아해.

ex. A : I don't like the singer. 나는 그 가수를 좋아하지 않아.
B : I **don't like** the singer, **either**. 나도 역시 그 가수를 좋아하지 않아.

의문문

> Do, Does + 주어 + 동사원형 ~ ?

주어가 1, 2인칭 단/복수, 3인칭 복수인 경우에 주어 앞에 **Do**를 붙이고, 주어가 3인칭 단수일 경우에는 주어 앞에 **Does**를 붙이고 문장 맨 뒤에 물음표(?)를 붙여 의문문을 만든다. 뒤에 오는 일반동사는 s나 es가 붙지 않은 동사 원형이 온다.

	단수			복수	
Do	I	동사원형~?		We	동사원형~?
	You		Do	You	
Does	He	동사원형 ~?		They	
	She				
	It				

ex. **Do** you (너는) like apples?　　　**Do** you (너희들은) like apples?

Does he like̶ apples?　　　**Do** they like apples?

Does she like̶ apples?

① 일반동사 의문문의 대답

일반동사 의문문의 대답은 **Yes/No**와 **do**와 **does**를 이용한다. 이 때도 주어는 대명사로 받고, 질문하는 사람과 대답하는 사람의 입장에 따라 주어가 달라질 수 있는 것에 주의한다.

Do ~?	Yes, ~ do. / No, ~ don't.
Does ~?	Yes, ~ does. / No, ~ doesn't.

ex. **Does** Tom like monkeys? Tom은 원숭이들 좋아하니?

　　 – Yes, he **does**. 응. 그래.　　　– No, he **doesn't**. 아니. 그렇지 않아.

　　 Do Tom and Paul play a computer game after school?

　　 – Yes, they **do**.　　　　　– No, they **don't**.

 의문문의 대답법은
be동사로 물어 보면 be동사로, Do/Does로 물어 보면 do/does로 대답한다.
ex. Is she a teacher? -Yes, she is.　　Does she teach English? -Yes, she does.

다음 ( ) 안에서 알맞은 말을 골라 동그라미 해 보자.

tell a lie 거짓말하다
dive 다이빙하다
socks 양말
credit card 신용카드
order 주문하다
feed 먹을 것을 주다
hen 암탉
about ~에 대하여
do exercise 운동하다

1 I (don't, doesn't) (tell, tells) a lie to my daddy.

2 We (don't, doesn't) (dive, dives) into the sea.

3 They (don't, doesn't) (buys, buy) a lot of socks.

4 It (don't, doesn't) (snows, snow).

5 He (don't, doesn't) (drive, drives) a truck.

6 You (don't, doesn't) (looks, look) like a model.

7 His mother (don't, doesn't) (have, has) a credit card.

8 We (don't, doesn't) (orders, order) five hamburgers.

9 She (don't, doesn't) (feed, feeds) the hens.

10 My daughters (doesn't, don't) (like, likes) to dance.

11 The monkey (don't, doesn't) (eat, eats) any fish.

12 Kevin (don't, doesn't) (rides, ride) a bike.

13 Sally and I (don't, doesn't) (talk, talks) about it.

14 The man (don't, doesn't) (does, do) exercise everyday.

15 The men (don't, doesn't) (take, takes) a taxi.

2

다음 ( ) 안에서 알맞은 말을 골라 동그라미 해 보자.

1 ((Do), Does) you ((know), knows) them?

2 (Do, Does) she (enters, enter) the room?

3 (Do, Does) her sister (sit, sits) on the bench?

4 (Do, Does) they (takes, take) pictures?

5 (Do, Does) he (come, comes) late?

6 (Do, Does) the students (like, likes) K-pop?

7 (Do, Does) Miss Kim (teach, teaches) history?

8 (Do, Does) the girl (invites, invite) her classmates?

9 (Do, Does) the women (sing, sings) well?

10 (Do, Does) the woman (pay, pays) for it?

11 (Do, Does) James (goes, go) on a picnic?

12 (Do, Does) they (draws, draw) cartoons?

13 (Do, Does) Judy and Mary (wears, wear) the jackets?

14 (Do, Does) Mrs. Bush (opens, open) her eyes?

15 (Do, Does) he (stand, stands) at the gate?

enter 들어가다
take a picture 사진을 찍다
late 늦게, 늦은
history 역사
invite 초대하다
classmate 같은 반 친구
cartoon 만화
gate 대문

다음 ( ) 안에서 알맞은 말을 골라 동그라미 해 보자.

learn 배우다
turn on ~을 켜다
shake hands with ~와
악수하다
tear 눈물을 흘리다
belong to ~에 속하다
bee 벌
collect 모으다
cashier 계산원
cash box 금고
like that 저것처럼

1 He (don't, doesn't) (moves, move) to London.

2 (Do, Does) he (pushes, push) the door?

3 She (don't, doesn't) (learn, learns) math.

4 (Do, Does) Paul (turn, turns) on the TV?

5 Tom (don't, doesn't) (shakes, shake) hands with others.

6 The baby (don't, doesn't) (tears, tear).

7 (Do, Does) your brothers (build, builds) the tower?

8 (Do, Does) Jane (wears, wear) a mask?

9 It (don't, doesn't) (belong, belongs) to Sumi.

10 (Do, Does) the bears (catches, catch) any fish?

11 You (don't, doesn't) (has, have) a pencil.

12 (Do, Does) your uncle (live, lives) in L.A?

13 The bees (don't, doesn't) (collect, collects) honey.

14 (Do, Does) the cashier (bring, brings) the cash box?

15 We (don't, doesn't) (does, do) like that.

4

다음 ( ) 안에서 알맞은 말을 골라 동그라미 해 보자.

1 I take a rest.

He takes a rest, (too, either).

2 We don't make a snowman.

They don't make a snowman, (too, either).

3 This book isn't very easy.

That book isn't very easy, (too, either).

4 He doesn't talk to me.

She doesn't talk to me, (too, either).

5 Peter Pan flies to the sky.

Wendy flies to the sky, (too, either).

6 She doesn't forget it.

He doesn't forget it, (too, either).

7 My mother loves chocolate cookies.

My father loves chocolate cookies, (too, either).

8 A tiger is an animal.

A lion is an animal, (too, either).

9 They don't study.

We don't study, (too, either).

10 Jenny answers the question.

Insu answers the question, (too, either).

take a rest 휴식을 취하다
snowman 눈사람
forget 잊다
animal 동물
wash the dishes 설거지를
하다
answer 대답하다
question 질문

다음 문장을 지시대로 바꿔 보자.

prepare tea 차를 만들다
concert 음악회
start 시작하다
grow 재배하다
understand 이해하다
go out 외출하다
capture 잡다
mosquito 모기
face 얼굴
carrot 당근
take off ~을 벗다

1 His mother prepares tea.

부정문 His mother *doesn't* *prepare* tea.

2 She opens her umbrella.

의문문 she her umbrella?

3 The concert starts at 8 o'clock.

부정문 The concert at 8 o'clock.

4 We grow a lot of tulips.

부정문 We a lot of tulips.

5 You(너는) understand your mother.

의문문 you your mother?

6 They go out.

부정문 They out.

7 He captures a mosquito.

부정문 He a mosquito.

8 It has a big face.

의문문 it a big face?

9 I hate carrots.

부정문 I carrots.

10 She takes off her cap.

의문문 she off her cap?

6

다음 문장을 지시대로 바꿔 보자.

1 They take the school bus.

부정문 They *don't* *take* the school bus.

2 Tom chats with her.

의문문 _____ Tom _____ with her?

3 It snows in Paris.

의문문 _____ it _____ in Paris?

4 She remembers his phone number.

부정문 She _____ his phone number.

5 You(너는) exercise every morning.

의문문 _____ you _____ every morning?

6 He chews the gum.

부정문 He _____ the gum.

7 We turn off the light.

부정문 We _____ off the light.

8 They look up at the time table.

의문문 _____ they _____ up at the time table?

9 The student solves the math problem.

의문문 _____ the student _____ the math problem?

10 My sisters set the table.

부정문 My sisters _____ the table.

chat with ~와 잡담하다
phone number 전화번호
exercise 운동하다
chew 씹다
turn off ~을 끄다
look up at ~을 올려다보다
time table 시간표
problem 문제
set the table (상을) 차리다

다음 문장을 지시대로 바꿔 보자.

frog 개구리
pond 연못
believe 믿다
iron 다림질하다
husband 남편
count 세다

1 He waits for us.

부정문   *He   doesn't   wait*   for us.

2 The frog sings at the pond.

의문문   at the pond?

3 They mix butter and sugar.

부정문   butter and sugar.

4 He and she believe Mr. Smith.

의문문   Mr. Smith?

5 Mrs. Park has a beautiful garden.

부정문   a beautiful garden.

6 She irons her husband' pants.

부정문   her husband' pants.

7 Matt builds his house.

의문문   his house?

8 You(너는) count to ten.

의문문   to ten?

9 His brothers work together.

부정문   together.

10 Mom makes a steak for me.

의문문   a steak for me?

다음 문장을 지시대로 바꿔 보자.

1 Tom and John trust the man.

의문문   *Do*   *Tom and John*   *trust*   the man?

2 They remember Thanksgiving Day.

부정문   Thanksgiving Day.

3 She eats out.

부정문   out.

4 Judy fries an egg.

의문문   an egg?

5 She forgets my phone number.

부정문   my phone number.

6 Paul plays the cello every day.

부정문   the cello every day.

7 Mom nags us.

부정문   us.

8 His parents buy a large farm.

의문문   a large farm?

9 We take a nap.

부정문   a nap.

10 He walks along the street.

부정문   along the street.

---

trust 신뢰하다
remember 기억하다
Thanksgiving Day 추수감사절
eat out 외식하다
stay in 나가지 않다
nag 잔소리하다
farm 농장
take a nap 낮잠을 자다
along ~을 따라서

다음 질문에 대답을 완성해 보자.

boil 끓이다
take 데리고 가다
theater 극장
truth 진실
French fries 감자 튀김
spell 철자를 쓰다
jump rope 줄넘기 하다

1 Does she boil it?

   – Yes, *she*   *does*   .

2 Does your mom take you to the theater?

   – No,   .

3 Does the cow eat grass?

   – Yes,   .

4 Do you(너는) tell the truth about that?

   – Yes,   .

5 Does the woman bake cookies?

   – No,   .

6 Do they have French fries?

   – Yes,   .

7 Does he call Jane?

   – Yes,   .

8 Do Joe and James come to the party?

   – No,   .

9 Do you(너는) spell your name?

   – No,   .

10 Does Jane jump rope?

   – No,   .

4

다음 문장의 빈칸에 too나 either를 써 보자.

healthy 건강한
COEX 종합전시관
(Convention & Exhibition)
receive 받다
loudly 큰 소리로

1 Tom loves sports.

I love sports, *too* .

2 She doesn't eat hamburgers.

He doesn't eat hamburgers, .

3 Mary wears a green T-shirt.

John wears a green T-shirt, .

4 My grandmother is healthy.

My grandmother is healthy, .

5 Jane doesn't go to COEX.

He doesn't go to COEX, .

6 I'm not busy now.

My sister isn't busy now, .

7 They receive an e-mail.

We receive an e-mail, .

8 She doesn't spend a lot of body lotion.

He doesn't spend a lot of body lotion, .

9 You(너는) speak loudly.

My cousin speaks loudly, .

10 I don't have a CD player.

He doesn't have a CD player, .

다음 밑줄 친 부분들 중에서 틀린 곳을 바르게 고쳐 써 보자.

bread and butter
버터 바른 빵
raise (위로) 올리다
homework 숙제
comic book 만화책
trust 신뢰하다

1 Does she <u>gives</u> bread and butter?
   give

2 He <u>don't raise</u> his hand.

3 They <u>sell not</u> new cars.

4 <u>Does</u> he <u>flies</u> the plane?

5 Mr. Hong <u>don't pass</u> through the gate.

6 <u>She do</u> her homework.

7 <u>Is</u> he <u>play</u> drum?

8 <u>Does</u> Jane <u>go</u> to the bank? – No, she <u>isn't</u>.

9 <u>Does</u> Ann's sisters <u>ride</u> their horses?

10 <u>Tom and John</u> <u>have not</u> their comic books.

11 <u>Does</u> she <u>meets</u> him in the coffee shop?

12 <u>Are</u> you(너는) <u>trust</u> your friend?

13 Does Mary <u>eat</u> an orange? – No, she <u>don't</u>.

14 <u>Does</u> he and you <u>want</u> to live in Seoul?

15 He <u>doesn't</u> sleep well in summer.
    She doesn't sleep well in summer, <u>too</u>.

2

다음 밑줄 친 부분들 중에서 **틀린** 곳을 바르게 고쳐 써 보자.

1 <u>Do</u> he <u>see</u> a lot of cars on the street?
Does

2 Bob <u>isn't</u> <u>pass</u> a ball.

3 <u>Do</u> the concert <u>begin</u> at 7 o'clock?

4 She <u>doesn't</u> <u>goes</u> hiking.

5 <u>Does</u> you(너는) <u>choose</u> the fresh watermelon? – Yes, I do.

6 I want something.
Tommy wants <u>something</u>, <u>either</u>.

7 <u>Are</u> they <u>tell</u> the truth?

8 Your <u>daughter</u> <u>has not</u> a bracelet.

9 He <u>doesn't</u> <u>worries</u> about his future.

10 Do my sisters <u>look</u> for a nice armchair? - Yes, they <u>are</u>.

11 <u>Does</u> Maria's students <u>memorize</u> 50 words in a day?

12 Judy and Jane <u>doesn't</u> <u>wax</u> their cars.

13 They <u>aren't</u> <u>leave</u> Seoul.

14 Does your brother <u>walks</u> into your room? – Yes, he <u>does</u>.

15 <u>Does</u> Henry go there? – Yes, he <u>is</u>.

travel 여행하다
Europe 유럽
choose 선택하다
anything 어떤 것
truth 진실
worry about ~에 대해
걱정하다
future 미래
armchair 팔걸이 의자
memorize 암기하다
leave 떠나다

다음 문장의 동사를 ○표 하고, 동사의 종류를 고른 후, 지시대로 바꿔 보자.
의문문은 대답도 완성해 보자.

take a lesson 수업을 듣다
pretty 매우
climb up (산에) 오르다
mountain 산
age 나이
be out of town 출장 중이다
ramen 라면
angry 화가 난

*be동사(am, are, is)가
 있는 문장의 부정문은
 be동사 뒤에 not을 붙이
 고, 의문문은 주어와
 be동사의 위치를 바꾸고
 문장 뒤에 ?만 붙이면
 된다.

1 I take a violin lesson. (be동사, 일반동사)

부정문   *I don't take*   a violin lesson.

2 She is pretty busy. (be동사, 일반동사)

의문문   pretty busy?   – No,   .

3 They climb up the mountain. (be동사, 일반동사)

부정문   up the mountain.

4 Sumi and Jane are your friends. (be동사, 일반동사)

부정문   your friends.

5 His age is 12. (be동사, 일반동사)

의문문   12?   – No,   .

6 His parents buy a toy. (be동사, 일반동사)

의문문   a toy?   – Yes,   .

7 Those books are yours. (be동사, 일반동사)

의문문   yours?   – No,   .

8 Dad is out of town. (be동사, 일반동사)

부정문   out of town.

9 He makes good ramen. (be동사, 일반동사)

의문문   good ramen?   – Yes,   .

10 You(너는) are angry. (be동사, 일반동사)

의문문   angry?   – No,   .

4

다음 문장의 동사를 ○표 하고, 동사의 종류를 고른 후, 지시대로 바꿔 보자.
의문문은 대답도 완성해 보자.

1 Suji brushes her teeth.   (be동사, 일반동사)

   의문문   *Does Suji brush* her teeth? – Yes, *she does* .

2 That is a rose.   (be동사, 일반동사)

   의문문   a rose?   – No,   .

3 Sam goes to the mall.   (be동사, 일반동사)

   의문문   to the mall? – Yes,   .

4 They are my hair bands.   (be동사, 일반동사)

   부정문   my hair bands.

5 The baby cries again.   (be동사, 일반동사)

   부정문   again.

6 The girl peels a pear.   (be동사, 일반동사)

   의문문   a pear?   – Yes,   .

7 This is his office.   (be동사, 일반동사)

   의문문   his office? – No,   .

8 She is my English teacher.   (be동사, 일반동사)

   부정문   my English teacher.

9 He rings the bell.   (be동사, 일반동사)

   부정문   the bell.

10 We play basketball.   (be동사, 일반동사)

   부정문   basketball.

---

brush 빗다
church 교회
hair band 머리밴드
smile 미소 짓다
again 다시
peel 껍질을 벗기다
ring (종을) 울리다
bell 종

01 다음 문장을 부정문으로 바꿀 때, 형태가 변하는 것은?

My mother <u>cooks</u> <u>dinner</u> <u>in</u> <u>the</u> <u>kitchen</u>.
              ①   ②   ③ ④   ⑤

02 다음 빈칸에 들어갈 말이 순서대로 바르게 짝지어진 것은?

A : _____ your father _____ the door?

B : No, he _____.

① Do - opens - don't
② Does - open - doesn't
③ Does - opens - don't
④ Do - open - doesn't
⑤ Does - open - don't

03 다음 문장을 부정문으로 바꿔 쓰시오.

I write an answer on the board.

→ _____

03

answer 답
board 칠판

04

swimmer 수영선수

정답 및 해설 p.6

04 다음 대화에서 빈칸에 들어갈 말로 알맞은 것은?

> A : Does Mr. Kim's daughter swim well?
>
> B : _____ She is a good swimmer.

① Yes, she does.

② Yes, she is.

③ No, she doesn't.

④ No, she isn't.

⑤ Yes, I do.

05 다음 문장 중 바른 것은?

① Mrs. Kim doesn't teaches English.

② They aren't win the game.

③ Does you run fast?

④ Does your mother sells many tomatoes?

⑤ Does he move to London?

06 다음 중 짝지어진 대화가 <u>틀린</u> 것은?

① A : Do they read a newspaper?
B : No, they don't.
② A : Do you play tennis?
B : Yes, I do.
③ A : Does she buy many dresses?
B : No, she doesn't.
④ A : Do you have a cellphone?
B : No, I don't.
⑤ A : Does Tom call Judy?
B : Yes, he do.

07 다음 중 빈칸에 들어갈 동사가 <u>다른</u> 것은?

① _____ she go shopping?
② _____ he a school teacher?
③ _____ he like potatoes?
④ _____ your father smoke?
⑤ _____ Miss Han eat breakfast?

08 다음 문장을 의문문으로 바꿔 쓰시오.

The students play baseball after school.

⇨ _____

09 다음 중 빈칸에 들어갈 말이 <u>다른</u> 것은?

① I like dogs. He likes dogs, _____.
② She washes the dishes.
   He washes the dishes, _____.
③ There is an apple on the table.
   There is a lemon on the table, _____.
④ You dance well.
   She dances well, _____.
⑤ A tiger is not a bird.
   A monkey is not a bird, _____.

10 다음 문장의 내용으로 추측할 수 있는 것은?

Peter doesn't wait for her.

Eric doesn't wait for her, either.

---

① Peter만 그녀를 기다린다.
② Eric만 그녀를 기다린다.
③ Peter와 Eric은 둘 다 그녀를 기다리지 않는다.
④ Peter와 Eric은 둘 다 그녀를 기다린다.
⑤ 오늘 밤 Peter와 Eric은 따로따로 그녀를 기다린다.

Quiz!

다음 문장을 지시대로 바꿔 보자.

1 You make your dress.

의문문

2 Mrs. Kim goes outside.

부정문

3 He takes a walk every day.

의문문

4 We clean our classroom.

부정문

5 Her children eat a snack between meals.

의문문

6 It rains.

의문문

7 He kicks a ball.

부정문

8 She and I send and receive text message. send and receive text message 문자를 주고 받다

부정문

9 The tree has a lot of apples.

의문문

10 They email Jane. email 이메일을 보내다

의문문

Unit 04

현재진행형

지금 하고 있는 일을 표현하며 「~하는 중이다.
~하고 있다」의 뜻을 나타낸다.
'be동사(am, are, is) + 동사원형 -ing'의
형태로 쓰인다.

현재진행형

현재진행형이란?

지금 하고 있는 일을 표현하는 말로, 「~하는 중이다, ~하고 있다」의 뜻이다.

1 현재진행형 만들기

> be동사(am, are, is) + 동사원형 ing

ex. I **am** study**ing**.　　　We **are** study**ing**.
He **is** study**ing**.　　　They **are** study**ing**.
She **is** study**ing**.

1 동사원형 –ing 형태 만드는 법

동사	공식	예
대부분의 동사	+ ing	cook - cooking
e로 끝나는 동사	e를 없애고 ing를 붙인다.	live - living
「단모음(1모음) + 단자음(1자음)」으로 끝나는 동사	마지막 자음을 하나 더 붙이고 + ing	sit - sitting run - running stop - stopping begin - beginning
예외1. 2음절 이상이면서 강세가 앞에 있는 동사	+ ing	lísten - listening ópen - opening vísit - visiting
예외2. w, x, y로 끝나는 동사	+ ing	show - showing fix - fixing say - saying
ie로 끝나는 동사	ie를 y로 고치고 + ing	die - dying lie - lying

부정문

be동사 뒤에 **not**을 붙여서 부정문을 만든다.

단수			복수		
I	am not	동사원형 ing~.	We	aren't	동사원형 ing~.
You	aren't		You		
He					
She	isn't		They		
It					
Tom					

ex. **I am not studying.**   **We are not studying.**

      He is not studying.   **They are not studying.**

      She is not studying.

 의문문

be동사를 주어 앞으로 보내고 문장 끝에 물음표(?) 붙여서 의문문을 만든다.

단수			복수		
Am	I	동사원형 ing~?	Are	We	동사원형 ing~?
Are	You			You	
Is	He			They	
	She				
	It				
	Tom				

ex. **Are you** (너는) **studying?**   **Are you** (너희들은) **studying?**

      Is he studying?   **Are they studying?**

      Is she studying?

대답은 **Yes/No**와 be동사를 이용한다.

ex. **Are you cleaning your room?**
      너는 너의 방을 치우고 있니?

      – **Yes, I am.**   – **No, I'm not.**
        응, 그래.   아니, 그렇지 않아.

> **Tip!** **소유, 감정, 인식을 나타내는 동사**
> have, know, like, love, hate, belong to, need, sound, feel, taste 등은 진행형을 만들 수 없다.
> *ex.* I love her. ~~I am loving her.~~
> 단, 동작을 나타낼 때는 진행형으로 사용이 가능하다.
> *ex.* He is having lunch. 그는 점심을 먹고 있다.

다음 문장의 시제를 고르고 두 문장의 뜻을 비교하여 우리말로 옮겨 보자.

draw 그리다
star 별
count 세다
Bulgogi 불고기

1 I study English. ((현재형), 현재진행형)

⇨ 나는 영어를 　　　　　　공부한다　　　　　　 .

I am studying English. (현재형, 현재진행형)

⇨ 나는 영어를 　　　　　　　　　　 .

2 You are drawing a picture. (현재형, 현재진행형)

⇨ 너는 그림을 　　　　　　　　　　 .

You draw a picture. (현재형, 현재진행형)

⇨ 너는 그림을 　　　　　　　　　　 .

3 He works hard. (현재형, 현재진행형)

⇨ 그는 열심히 　　　　　　　　　　 .

He is working hard. (현재형, 현재진행형)

⇨ 그는 열심히 　　　　　　　　　　 .

4 My sister counts stars with Jane. (현재형, 현재진행형)

⇨ 나의 여동생은 Jane과 함께 별을 　　　　　　　　　　 .

My sister is counting stars with Jane. (현재형, 현재진행형)

⇨ 나의 여동생은 Jane과 함께 별을 　　　　　　　　　　 .

5 She is cooking Bulgogi in the kitchen. (현재형, 현재진행형)

⇨ 그녀는 부엌에서 불고기를 　　　　　　　　　　 .

She cooks Bulgogi in the kitchen. (현재형, 현재진행형)

⇨ 그녀는 부엌에서 불고기를 　　　　　　　　　　 .

2

다음 동사를 –ing 형태로 바꾼 것이다. 알맞은 것을 골라 동그라미 해 보자.

1 run   (runing, (running))   2 open   (opening, openning)

3 stand   (standing, standding)   4 drop   (droping, dropping)

5 try   (triing, trying)   6 tie   (tieing, tying)

7 lie   (lieing, lying)   8 play   (playing, plaiing)

9 get   (getting, geting)   10 ride   (rideing, riding)

11 write   (writeing, writing)   12 die   (dieing, dying)

13 study   (studying, studing)   14 wax   (waxing, waxxing)

15 stop   (stoping, stopping)   16 watch   (watching, watcheing)

17 speak   (speaking, speakking)   18 cry   (crying, criing)

19 chat   (chating, chatting)   20 work   (workking, working)

21 draw   (drawing, drawwing)   22 visit   (visitting, visiting)

23 come   (coming, comeing)   24 use   (using, useing)

25 listen   (listenning, listening)   26 wash   (washning, washing)

27 begin   (begining, beginning)   28 wait   (waitting, waiting)

29 eat   (eating, eatting)   30 sing   (sing, singing)

lie 누워있다, 거짓말하다
tie 묶다
die 죽다

다음 동사를 –ing 형태로 바꿔 보자.

ski 스키를 타다
say 말하다
pay 지불하다
win 승리하다

1	ski	*skiing*	2	begin
3	teach		4	say
5	tie		6	have
7	draw		8	drive
9	fix		10	mix
11	sit		12	fly
13	tear		14	put
15	swim		16	open
17	die		18	cut
19	enjoy		20	wash
21	listen		22	dance
23	tell		24	lie
25	come		26	stop
27	wait		28	visit
29	win		30	fry

4

다음 문장을 현재진행형으로 바꿔 보자.

1 I fly a plane.

⇨ I _am flying_ a plane.

2 Judy and David cut a big tree.

⇨ Judy and David _____ a big tree.

3 We water the flower bed.

⇨ We _____ the flower bed.

4 Sara sits on the couch.

⇨ Sara _____ on the couch.

5 He waxes his car.

⇨ He _____ his car.

6 A snake eats a frog.

⇨ A snake _____ a frog.

7 You make a salad.

⇨ You _____ a salad.

8 Your friend looks after Minho.

⇨ Your friend _____ after Minho.

9 This bus goes very slowly.

⇨ This bus _____ very slowly.

10 Some boys play Taekwondo in the gym.

⇨ Some boys _____ Taekwondo in the gym.

---

water 물을 주다
flower bed 꽃밭
couch 소파
salad 샐러드
look after 돌보다
play Taekwondo
태권도를 하다

시제를 고른 후 |보기|의 단어들을 알맞은 형태로 바꿔 문장의 빈칸을 채워 보자.

snore 코를 골다
take a rest 휴식을 취하다
eagle 독수리
fly 날다
in the air 공중에서
quit 끊다
lie 거짓말하다
matter 일, 사건

|보기|	make	snore	snow	play	fly
	skate	quit	lie	take	look at

1 지금 눈이 오고 있다. (현재형, (현재진행형))

⇨ It _is snowing_ now.

2 수진이와 나는 Ann의 드레스를 만들고 있다. (현재형, 현재진행형)

⇨ Sujin And I _____ Ann's dress.

3 그는 몇 몇 나비들을 바라보고 있는 중이다. (현재형, 현재진행형)

⇨ He _____ some butterflies.

4 나는 친구들과 농구를 한다. (현재형, 현재진행형)

⇨ I _____ basketball with my friends.

5 너의 삼촌은 코를 골고 있다. (현재형, 현재진행형)

⇨ Your uncle _____ .

6 그녀의 여동생들은 휴식을 취하는 중이다. (현재형, 현재진행형)

⇨ Her sisters _____ a rest.

7 독수리가 공중에서 날고 있다. (현재형, 현재진행형)

⇨ An eagle _____ in the air.

8 나의 아빠는 담배를 끊으신다. (현재형, 현재진행형)

⇨ My daddy _____ smoking.

9 Nancy는 지금 그 일에 대해 거짓말을 하고 있다. (현재형, 현재진행형)

⇨ Nancy _____ about the matter now.

10 그들은 아이스링크에서 스케이트를 탄다. (현재형, 현재진행형)

⇨ They _____ in the ice rink.

2

시제를 고른 후 |보기|의 단어들을 알맞은 형태로 바꿔 문장의 빈칸을 채워 보자.

| 보기 | watch   use   carry   move   hunt |
| tie   die   keep   blow   walk |

blow 불다
south 남쪽
move around 주위를 돌다
use 사용하다
living room 거실
old and used thing 중고품
die 죽다
keep 보관하다
leftover 남은 음식
chicken 닭고기
shoelaces 운동화 끈
hunt 사냥하다
forest 숲

1 그는 매일 도서관에 걸어간다. ((현재형), 현재진행형)
⇨ He   *walks*   to the library every day.

2 바람이 남쪽으로부터 불고 있다. (현재형, 현재진행형)
⇨ The wind   from the south.

3 달은 지구의 주위를 돈다. (현재형, 현재진행형)
⇨ The moon   around the earth.

4 우리는 지금 그 수박들을 나르고 있다. (현재형, 현재진행형)
⇨ We   the watermelons now.

5 그녀가 거실에서 TV를 보고 있다. (현재형, 현재진행형)
⇨ She   TV in the living room.

6 그와 그녀는 중고품을 사용한다. (현재형, 현재진행형)
⇨ He and she   old and used things.

7 그 늙은 사자는 죽어가고 있다. (현재형, 현재진행형)
⇨ The old lion   .

8 엄마는 냉장고에 치킨 남은 것을 보관한다. (현재형, 현재진행형)
⇨ Mom   leftover chicken in the
refrigerator

9 나의 여동생은 그녀의 운동화 끈을 묶고 있다. (현재형, 현재진행형)
⇨ My sister   her shoelaces.

10 Matt는 숲에서 사냥하고 있다. (현재형, 현재진행형)
⇨ Matt   in the forest.

다음 문장을 지시대로 바꿔 보자.

sew 바느질하다
sweep out 쓸어내다
shine 빛나다
vegetable 야채
textbook 교과서

1 You(너는) are enjoying the party.

의문문 *Are*　*you*　*enjoying*　the party?

2 Your daughter is cleaning the table.

부정문 　　　　　　　　　　　　the table.

3 I am dreaming now.

부정문 　　　　　　　　now.

4 My aunt is sewing her socks.

의문문 　　　　　　　her socks?

5 She is sweeping out the market.

의문문 　　　　　　　out the market?

6 The stars are shining.

부정문 　　　　　　　　.

7 He is cooking vegetables.

의문문 　　　　　　　vegetables?

8 They are reading their textbooks.

의문문 　　　　　　　their textbooks?

9 Koreans are wearing red shirts.

의문문 　　　　　　　red shirts?

10 The kid is eating an ice cream.

부정문 　　　　　　　an ice cream.

4

다음 질문에 Yes와 No로 시작하는 대답을 완성해 보자.

1 Is she drinking a lot of soda pop?

– Yes, *she* *is* .

2 Are they watering the flowers?

– No, .

3 Are the boys looking around the town?

– Yes, .

4 Are you(너는) shopping at the department store?

– No, .

5 Is it raining outside?

– Yes, .

6 Is he holding her hand?

– Yes, .

7 Are Tom and Jim circling in red ink?

– No, .

8 Is it getting dark?

– No, .

9 Is your son lying on the bed?

– Yes, .

10 Are the boys practicing baseball?

– No, .

soda pop 음료수
water 물을 주다
soccer 축구
look around 둘러보다
department store 백화점
circle 동그라미를 그리다
hold 잡다

다음 문장의 시제를 고른 후, 지시대로 바꾸고, 의문문은 대답도 완성해 보자.

hate 싫어하다
snake 뱀
book report 독후감

1 You(너는) hate snakes.　　　　　　　　(**현재형**, 현재진행형)

　　의문문　　*Do you hate*　　snakes?　– Yes, 　*I do*　.

2 The sun is rising now.　　　　　　　　(현재형, 현재진행형)

　　의문문　　　　　　　　　now?　– No, 　　　　　.

3 Mom is washing my uniform.　　　　　　(현재형, 현재진행형)

　　부정문　　　　　　　　my uniform.

4 The bus goes slowly.　　　　　　　　　(현재형, 현재진행형)

　　의문문　　　　　　　slowly?　– Yes, 　　　　　.

5 He is listening to the radio.　　　　　　(현재형, 현재진행형)

　　부정문　　　　　　　to the radio.

6 People run around the lake.　　　　　　(현재형, 현재진행형)

　　부정문　　　　　　　around the lake.

7 Your parents are shopping.　　　　　　(현재형, 현재진행형)

　　의문문　　　　　　　　– No, 　　　　　.

8 Jane stands up.　　　　　　　　　　　(현재형, 현재진행형)

　　의문문　　　　　　　up?　– Yes, 　　　　　.

9 I am writing a book report.　　　　　　(현재형, 현재진행형)

　　부정문　　　　　　　a book report.

10 The man sleeps in a tent.　　　　　　(현재형, 현재진행형)

　　의문문　　　　　　　in a tent?　– No, 　　　　　.

2

다음 문장의 시제를 고른 후, 지시대로 바꾸고, 의문문은 대답도 완성해 보자. (be동사를 사용한 문장과 현재형문장도 있으니 주의할 것)

1 She is waxing a ball.　　　　　(현재형, [현재진행형])

의문문　　*Is she waxing*　　a ball?　　– Yes,　　*she is*　　.

2 We are working for the company.　　(현재형, 현재진행형)

부정문　　　　　　　　　　for the company.

3 He snores loudly.　　　　　　(현재형, 현재진행형)

의문문　　　　　　loudly?　　– No,　　　　.

4 Your dad is playing tennis.　　　(현재형, 현재진행형)

부정문　　　　　　　　tennis.

5 The girls ski on the hill.　　　(현재형, 현재진행형)

부정문　　　　　　　　on the hill.

6 The lady is trying on it.　　　(현재형, 현재진행형)

의문문　　　　　　it?　　– Yes,　　　　.

7 You(너는) worry about that.　　(현재형, 현재진행형)

의문문　　　　　　that?　　– Yes,　　　　.

8 My sisters are dancing to music.　　(현재형, 현재진행형)

부정문　　　　　　　　to music.

9 The penguin swims well.　　　(현재형, 현재진행형)

부정문　　　　　　　　well.

10 They have supper.　　　　　(현재형, 현재진행형)

의문문　　　　　　supper?　　– No,　　　　.

wax 윤을 내다
snore 코를 골다
company 회사
work for 근무하다
loudly 큰 소리로
worry 걱정하다
future 미래
penguin 펭귄
catch 잡다

다음 밑줄 친 부분들 중에서 틀린 곳을 바르게 고쳐 써 보자.

need 필요하다
want 원하다
train station 기차역
tour 여행하다
Africa 아프리카
repair 고치다, 수선하다

1 나는 말을 타는 중이다.
I <u>riding</u> <u>a</u> horse.
am riding

2 그녀는 지우개가 필요하다.
She <u>is needing</u> <u>an</u> eraser.

3 우리는 잔디 위에서 점심을 먹고 있다.
We <u>are</u> <u>eat</u> lunch on the grass.

4 그는 지금 수학을 가르치고 있니?
<u>Does</u> he <u>teaching</u> math now?

5 너는 컴퓨터로 점검하고 있니?
<u>Are</u> you checking on computer? Yes, I <u>do</u>.

6 수민이는 돌아가기를 원한다.
Sumin <u>is wanting</u> to <u>go</u> back.

7 사람들이 기차역에서 기다리고 있다.
People <u>is</u> <u>waiting</u> at the train station.

8 그들은 다시 아프리카를 여행하고 있는 중이다.
They <u>touring</u> Africa <u>again</u>.

9 나의 여동생은 그녀의 목걸이를 고치고 있다.
My sister <u>repairs</u> her <u>necklace</u>.

10 나는 남동생에게 전화를 걸고 있다.
I <u>calling</u> <u>my</u> brother.

다음 밑줄 친 부분들 중에서 틀린 곳을 바르게 고쳐 써 보자.

1 그녀는 불고기를 요리하고 있니?
Does she cooking Bulgogi?
Is

2 Joe는 사진을 찍고 있지 않다.
Joe is not take a picture.

3 가끔 그 나이 든 부인은 그녀의 아들의 얼굴을 잊어 버린다.
Sometimes the old lady is forgetting her son's face.

4 누가 내 연필을 사용하고 있니?
Who is use my pencil?

5 그는 지금 아침을 먹고 있다.
He having breakfast now.

6 나는 건강을 위해 녹차를 마신다.
I am drinking green tea for health.

7 그들은 밖에서 놀고 있니?
Do they playing outside?

8 나의 삼촌은 식당에서 식사하고 계시니?   – 아니오 , 그렇지 않아요.
Is my uncle having dinner in the dinning room?
– No, he doesn't.

9 Mary와 Ann은 화장을 하고 있다.
Mary and Ann is wear makeup.

10 나는 Jane을 비웃고 있는 것이 아니다.
I don't laughing at Jane.

forget 잊다
exercise 운동하다
wear makeup 화장하다
laugh at ~를 비웃다

실전Test

01 다음 문장은 현재진행형의 부정문이다. 공통으로 들어갈 것은?

01
pork 돼지고기

> · Sam's sister _____ running to school.
>
> · Sam _____ cooking the pork.

① amn't   ② aren't

③ isn't   ④ don't

⑤ doesn't

02 다음 중 동사원형과 −ing 형태가 바르게 짝지어진 것은?

① eat - eatting

② die - dieing

③ run - runing

④ smile - smileing

⑤ swim - swimming

03 다음 우리말을 영어로 쓸 때, 빈칸에 알맞은 말은?

03
lie ① 거짓말
 ex. tell a lie 거짓말하다
 ② 눕다

> 수진은 지금 바닥에 누워 있는 중이다.
>
> → Sujin is _____ on the floor now.

① lie   ② lies

③ lieing   ④ lyeing

⑤ lying

04 다음 질문에 대한 대답으로 알맞은 것은?

> A : Is he reading a newspaper?
>
> B : _____

① Yes, she does.　　② Yes, he is.
③ He isn't.　　④ He is.
⑤ No, he doesn't.

05 다음 문장을 부정문으로 바꿔 쓰시오.

> He is working at his office.
>
> → _____

06 다음 문장 중 바른 것은?

① Do you playing the piano?
② I don't learning music.
③ Mr. Kim is having dinner.
④ She studying English.
⑤ Are the girls cook in the kitchen.

07 다음 빈칸에 들어갈 말로 알맞은 것은?

> They are skating in the pond _____.

① yesterday
② tomorrow
③ tomorrow morning
④ now
⑤ last night

더 알아보기

07

pond 연못

[08–09] 다음 문장을 현재형으로 바꿔 쓰시오.

08

> I am dancing in my room.
>
> → _____

09

> She is washing her hands.
>
> → _____

10 다음 문장을 우리말로 옮길 때, 바르지 <u>않은</u> 것은?

10

do one's homework
숙제를 하다

① He is driving a car now.

→ 그는 지금 차를 운전하고 있다.

② The baby is sleeping well.

→ 그 아기는 잘 잔다.

③ Tom is doing his homework.

→ Tom은 그의 숙제를 하고 있다.

④ She sells many strawberries.

→ 그녀는 많은 딸기를 판다.

⑤ I am painting my house.

→ 나는 나의 집을 칠하고 있다.

다음 |보기|의 단어를 알맞은 형태로 바꿔 문장의 빈칸에 써 보자.

|보기|	repair	drive	mix	catch	help
	jog	wash	practice	cross	enjoy

1 그녀는 차를 운전한다.

She   a car.

2 수정이는 설거지를 하고 있다.

Sujung   the dishes.

3 일찍 일어나는 새가 벌레를 잡는다.

The early bird   the worm.

4 나는 파티를 즐기고 있다.

I   the party.

5 한 노인과 그의 부인이 길을 건너고 있는 중이다.

An old man and his wife   the street.

6 많은 사람들이 Central Park에서 조깅하고 있다.

A lot of people   at the Central Park.

7 Tom은 그의 컴퓨터를 고치는 중이다.

Tom   his computer.

8 엄마는 밀가루와 설탕을 섞고 계신다.

Mother   flour and sugar.

9 그는 항상 노인들을 돕는다.

He always   old men.

10 Jane과 그녀의 아버지는 홀에서 연습하고 있다. practice 연습하다

Jane and her father   in the hall.

- # Review Test 1
- # 내신대비 1

01 다음 ( ) 안에서 알맞은 동사를 골라 동그라미 해 보자.

1 There (is, are) twenty apples in the box.

2 There (is, are) nothing left on his bag.

3 There (is, are) a little cake in the refrigerator.

4 There (is, are) 700 workers in this factory.

5 There (is, are) a university in the city.

02 주어진 단어를 이용하여 우리말에 알맞게 빈칸을 채워 보자.

1   at the taxi stand.
택시 정류장에 두 사람이 있다.   (two men)

2   behind our house.
우리 집 뒤에 산이 없다.   (a mountain)

3   in the basket.
바구니 안에 약간의 빵이 있다.   (some bread)

4   in the bowl.
사발 안에 우유가 거의 없다.   (little milk)

5   by my computer.
나의 컴퓨터 옆에 책과 펜이 있다.   (a book and a pen)

○3 다음 문장을 지시대로 바꿔 보고 의문문은 대답도 완성해 보자.

1 There is a fish on the cutting board. cutting board 도마

의문문 _____ on the cutting board?

Yes, _____ .

2 There are ten boys in the classroom.

의문문 _____ in the classroom?

No, _____ .

3 There are a lot of taxis on the street.

부정문 _____ on the street.

4 There is a lot of honey.

의문문 _____ ? Yes, _____ .

5 There are six cups on the table.

부정문 _____ on the table.

6 There is a lot of cheese in the kitchen.

부정문 _____ in the kitchen.

7 There is a girl among the boys.

부정문 _____ among the boys.

8 There are three stories in this book.

의문문 _____ in this book?

No, _____ .

9 There are two cellphones in his pocket.

부정문 _____ in his pocket.

10 There is a river in this town.

의문문 _____ in this town?

No, _____ .

01 다음 (   ) 안에서 알맞은 동사의 형태를 골라 동그라미 해 보자.

1 He (study, studies) science.

2 She (like, likes) movies.

3 I (know, knows) the boy.

4 Tom (go, goes) to middle school.

5 The dog (have, has) a long tail.

6 We (play, plays) soccer.

7 Susan (wash, washes) her hands.

02 다음 (   ) 안에 알맞은 주어를 골라 동그라미 해 보자.

1 (He, I) needs a cup.

2 (She, They) sees a movie.

3 (You, The boy) swim well.

4 (Dad, We) comes late.

5 (Jane, Tom and Jane) study hard.

6 (Uncle, They) lives in New York.

7 (He, I) keep a dog.

03 다음 ( ) 안의 동사를 현재형으로 알맞게 바꿔 보자.

1 My sister   a shower everyday. (take)

2 Jane   the piano well. (play)

3 I   homework before dinner. (do)

4 He   a Coke. (drink)

5 The baby   loud. (cry)

6 Dad   to the park with the dog. (go)

7 My jacket   five buttons. (have)

8 They   a thief. (catch)

9 Tom   swimming. (enjoy)

10 Mr. Smith   baggage at the airport. (carry)

11 The chicken   good. (taste)

12 Jake   the washing machine. (fix)   washing machine 세탁기

13 Swallows   away in fall. (fly)

14 The old men   slowly. (speak)

15 Susan   to be a teacher. (hope)

01 다음 (   ) 안에서 알맞은 말을 골라 동그라미 해보자.

1 She (don't, doesn't) (know, knows) the man.

2 He (don't, doesn't) (has, have) money.

3 I (don't, doesn't) (eat, eats) carrot.

4 They (don't, doesn't) (play, plays) together.

5 Susan (don't, doesn't) (study, studies) in the library.

02 다음 (   ) 안에서 알맞은 말을 골라 동그라미 해보자.

1 (Do, Does) he (speak, speaks) English?

2 (Do, Does) you (write, writes) a diary?

3 (Do, Does) Bill (like, likes) skiing?

4 (Do, Does) they (live, lives) in Seoul?

5 (Do, Does) your mom (drive, drives) a car?

03 다음 (   ) 안에서 알맞은 말을 골라 동그라미 해보자.

1 He likes soccer.
    I like soccer, (too, either).

2 Tom keeps a dog.
    Jane keeps a dog, (too, either).

3 She doesn't know the boy.
    I don't know the boy, (too, either).

04 다음 문장을 지시대로 바꿀 때, 빈칸에 알맞게 말을 써 보자.

1 He sleeps on the sofa.

의문문 _____ on the sofa?

Yes, _____ .

2 They go shopping together.

의문문 _____ shopping together?

Yes, _____ .

3 Susan likes math.

부정문 _____ math.

4 I have a brother.

부정문 _____ a brother.

5 She keeps a dog.

의문문 _____ a dog?   No, _____ .

6 Tom knows the news.

부정문 _____ the news.

7 You(너는) have a coin.

의문문 _____ a coin?   No, _____ .

05 우리말에 알맞게 빈칸을 채워 보자.

1 Bill has a bike.   Bill은 자전거를 가지고 있어.

Tom has a bike, _____ .   Tom도 자전거를 가지고 있어.

2 Jane doesn't eat pork.   Jane은 돼지고기를 안 먹어.

I don't eat pork, _____ .   나도 돼지고기를 안 먹어.

3 His uncle lives in America.   그의 삼촌은 미국에 살아.

My aunt lives in America, _____ .   내 고모도 미국에 살아.

01 다음은 현재진행형 문장들이다. (   ) 안에서 알맞은 동사를 골라 동그라미 해 보자.

1 He (am, is, are) (eats, eating) bread.

2 I (am, is, are) (come, coming) home.

3 They (am, is, are) (sing, singing) now.

4 She (am, is, are) (driving, driveing) a car.

5 We (am, is, are) (chating, chatting) now.

02 우리말에 알맞게 빈칸을 채워 보자.

1 _____ a pen. choose 고르다

그는 펜을 고르고 있는 중이다.

2 _____ English.

나는 영어를 배우고 있는 중이다.

3 _____ yoga. do yoga 요가를 하다

엄마는 요가를 하는 중이다.

4 _____ in the sea. sail 항해하다

그들은 바다에서 항해하고 있는 중이다.

5 _____ with Bill. talk 이야기하다

Tom은 Bill과 함께 이야기하고 있는 중이다.

03 다음 문장을 지시대로 바꾸고 의문문은 대답도 완성해 보자.

1 He is taking a test.

부정문 _____ a test.

2 She is cutting a cake.

의문문 _____ a cake?   Yes, _____ .

3 I am cooking with mom.

부정문 _____ with mom.

4 They are playing soccer.

의문문 _____ soccer?   Yes, _____ .

5 We are going to school.

부정문 _____ to school.

6 Tom is teaching math.

의문문 _____ math?   No, _____ .

7 It is raining now.

부정문 _____ now.

8 It is snowing there.

의문문 _____ there?   No, _____ .

9 The horses are running together.

부정문 _____ together.

10 Your sister is buying some bread.

의문문 _____ any bread?

No, _____ .

01 다음 중 is가 필요한 곳은?

① There _____ two books on the desk.
② There _____ many people on the street.
③ There _____ some coins in my pocket.
④ There _____ a hairpin in her hand.
⑤ There _____ 10 apples in the basket.

02 다음 빈칸에 알맞은 것은?

There are _____ on the table.

① a cup
② some bread
③ an egg
④ some milk
⑤ some cookies

03 주어진 단어를 바르게 배열하여 문장을 완성해 보자.

his room, a bed, is, in, there

⇨ _____

_____

04 다음 중 어법상 옳은 것은?

① There is two houses on the hill.
② There are a lot of milk.
③ There is four rooms in my house.
④ There are a lot of books in the library.
⑤ There are an old bus.

05 주어진 문장을 부정문으로 만들어 보자.

There are a few trees in the park.

⇨ _____

_____

a few 약간의

06 다음 의문문의 대답으로 알맞은 것은?

> Is there a doll on the bed?

① Yes, it is.
② Yes, there is.
③ No, there is.
④ Yes, there are.
⑤ No, you are not.

07 우리말을 영어로 바꾼 것입니다. 다음 중 **틀린** 곳을 바르게 고쳐 보자.

> 나의 정원에 약간의 장미들이 있습니다.
> → They are some roses in my garden.

_____ ⇨ _____

08 주어가 3인칭 단수 일 때의 동사의 현재형으로 맞는 것은?

① ask-askes
② take-takees
③ see-sees
④ teach-teachs
⑤ stay-staies

09 빈칸에 알맞은 것은?

> They _____ fishing.
> Tom _____ everyday.
> She _____ all day.

① go - works - dances
② goes - work - dances
③ go - works - dance
④ goes - works - dance
⑤ go - work - dances

10 다음 빈칸에 들어갈 말로 알맞지 **않은** 것은?

> _____ watches the soccer game after dinner.

① He
② She
③ Dad
④ I
⑤ Tom

11 다음 중 올바른 문장은?

① She have a lot of friends.
② I likes apples.
③ Mr. Lee teaches art.
④ They cleans the house on weekend.
⑤ Jimmy and Bill plays together.

12 다음 중 어법상 옳지 <u>않은</u> 것은?

① Tom doesn't speaks English.
② He doesn't play basketball.
③ She doesn't drink tea.
④ It doesn't have meat.
⑤ He doesn't eat it.

meat 고기

13 다음 우리말에 알맞은 것은?

> He _____ classical music.
> 그는 클래식 음악을 좋아하지 않는다.

① don't like
② don't likes
③ isn't like
④ isn't likes
⑤ doesn't like

14 다음 빈칸에 순서대로 들어갈 것은?

> • _____ you have lunch?
> – Yes, I _____
> • _____ your dad play golf?
> – Yes, he _____.

① Do /do - Do /do
② Are /are - am
③ Do /do - Does /does
④ Does /does - Do /do
⑤ Does /does - Does /does

15 <u>틀린</u> 곳을 찾아 바르게 고쳐 보자.

> Mary doesn't goes to bed at 10 p.m.

_____ ⇨ _____

16 다음 우리말에 알맞은 것들로 짝지어진 것은?

> _____ she _____ a dog?
>
> 그녀는 개를 기르니?

① Do - keep
② Does - keep
③ Do - keeps
④ Does - keeps
⑤ Does - keeping

17 주어진 문장을 부정문으로 바르게 바꾼 것은?

> They go to church.

① They aren't go to church.
② They isn't go to church.
③ They don't go to church.
④ They don't goes to church.
⑤ They doesn't go to church.

18 다음 의문문의 대답으로 알맞은 것은?

> Does Tom have a sister ?

① Yes, he has.
② No, he hasn't.
③ Yes, he does.
④ No, he don't
⑤ Yes, he have.

19 주어진 동사의 –ing 형이 옳은 것은?

① eat-eating
② chat-chating
③ live-liveing
④ lie-liing
⑤ sing-singging

20 다음 빈칸에 들어갈 말을 고르면?

> He _____ _____ now.

① is, study
② is, studying
③ am, study
④ are, study
⑤ are, studying

21 다음 문장을 현재진행형으로 바꿔 보자.

> Jane plays the cello.

⇨ _____

22 다음 문장을 부정문으로 옳게 바꾼 것은?

> I am reading a book.

① I not am reading a book.
② I don't reading a book.
③ I am not reading a book.
④ I am don't reading a book.
⑤ I am reading not a book.

23 다음 의문문의 대답으로 알맞은 것은?

> Are they singing a song?

① Yes, they do.
② No, they don't.
③ Yes, they aren't.
④ No, they aren't.
⑤ No, they are

24 빈칸에 들어갈 말로 알맞게 짝지어진 것은?

> _____ you _____
> your classroom?

① Are-cleaning
② Are-clean
③ Do-cleaning
④ Do-cleans
⑤ Is-cleaning

25 주어진 동사를 이용하여 우리말에 알맞게 빈칸을 채워 보자.

> · She _____ everyday.
> (jog)
> 그녀는 매일 조깅한다.
> · She _____ now.
> (jog)
> 그녀는 지금 조깅하고 있다.

Unit 05

형용사

명사 바로 앞에 와서 명사를 꾸며 주거나,
be동사와 함께 쓰여 주어를
보충 설명해 주는 역할을 한다.

05 형용사

형용사란?

명사를 꾸며 주거나 주어를 보충·설명해 주는 말이다.

1 형용사의 종류

상태	색깔	숫자	맛	날씨
beautiful cute famous fresh great handsome lovely new nice	black blue brown gray green pink purple violet white yellow	one two three four five six seven eight nine ten	bitter hot salty sour sweet	warm hot cool sunny cloudy rainy snowy windy foggy stormy muggy

famous 유명한
fresh 신선한
great 훌륭한
brown 갈색의
gray 회색의
purple 보라색의
violet 자주색의
bitter 쓴 맛의
hot 매운 맛의
salty 짠 맛의
sour 신 맛의
sweet 달콤한
cool 시원한
cloudy 흐린
foggy 안개 긴
muggy 무더운
stormy 폭풍우 치는
sunny 화창한
windy 바람이 부는

Tip! 형용사는 많이 알면 알수록 편리하다. 104쪽에서는 형용사의 종류별로 분류하였고, 106쪽과 107쪽에서는 외우기 쉽도록 반대의 의미를 가진 형용사 별로 분류해 놓았으니 모두 부지런히 외워 두도록 하자.

2 형용사의 용법

1 한정적 용법

A. 쓰임

명사 바로 앞에 와서 명사를 꾸며주는 역할을 한다. 주로 "～한"으로 해석된다.

ex. a **pretty** **girl**   예쁜 소녀
　　　형용사　명사

B. 형용사의 위치

▶ 명사만 있는 경우

형용사 + 명사

ex. a **good** boy   착한 소년
      형용사   명사

▶ 부사가 함께 오는 경우

a/an/the + 부사 + 형용사 + 명사

a/an + 부사 + 형용사 + 명사 순으로 온다.

ex. a very **good** boy   매우 착한 소년
      부사   형용사 명사

단, 복수일 경우는 **a/an**을 붙이지 않는다.

ex. very good boys   매우 착한 소년들
    ~~a very good boys.~~

▶ 소유격이 함께 오는 경우

소유격 + 형용사 + 명사

ex. my **good** friend   나의 좋은 친구
    소유격 형용사 명사

Tip! 형용사가 명사를 꾸며준다는 말은 어떤 의미일까?

예를 들어 설명해 보자.
엄마가 휴대폰을 사주셨어요. 그것은 그냥 평범한 휴대폰이었지만, 여기에 내가 스티커도 붙이고 예쁜 고리도 달았다면 어떻게 변했을까? '멋진' 휴대폰이 되었겠지?
이 때 '멋진'이 핸드폰이 어떤 상태인지 알려준다. 그래서 '멋진'이 명사인 핸드폰을 꾸며주는 역할을 하는 것이다.
ex. a cell phone 휴대폰
    a nice cell phone 멋진 휴대폰

Tip! 형용사의 배열순서는

첫 글자를 따서 '지관수대 형신명'으로 외우도록 한다. 대개의 경우 이렇게 많은 형용사를 한꺼번에 사용하는 경우는 거의 없지만 그 중 일부를 사용할 때 이 순서가 필요하다.

▶ 형용사가 2개 이상일 경우

지시형용사 / 관사 + 수량 + 대 / 소 + 형상 + 신 / 구 + 명사

지시형용사/관사	수량	대/소	형상	신/구	명사
these	two	big	round	new	buildings
이	두 개의	크고	둥근	새로운	건물들

② 서술적 용법

A. 쓰임

주어를 보충 설명해주는 역할을 한다. be동사와 함께 쓰여 '~하다'로 해석된다.

ex. <u>Jane</u> <u>is</u> <u>kind</u>. Jane은 친절하다. (Jane = kind)
　　　주어　be동사　형용사

> **Tip!** '친절하다'는 동사가 아니라 '친절한 + 이다'로 이루어진 말이다. 우리말에서는 '친절한 + 이다'의 순서로 오지만 영어에서는 '이다 + 친절한'의 순서로 온다. 그러므로 서술적 용법은 'be동사+형용사'가 된다.

▶ 서로 반대의 뜻을 가진 형용사들 1

▶ 서로 반대의 뜻을 가진 형용사들 2

'un'을 붙여 반대되는 의미를 가진 형용사를 만드는 경우가 있다.

ex. kind 친절한 ↔ unkind 불친절한 　　happy 행복한 ↔ unhappy 불행한

　　 able 가능한 ↔ unable 불가능한 　　wise 현명한 ↔ unwise 현명하지 못한

▶ 서로 반대의 뜻을 가진 형용사들 3

B. 감각동사 + 형용사

사람의 감각을 나타내는 동사(look, sound, smell, feel, taste···) 뒤에는 형용사가 온다.

look	~처럼 보이다	sound	~처럼 들리다
smell	~한 냄새가나다	feel	~하게 느끼다
taste	~한 맛이 나다		

ex. He **looks** tired.   그는 피곤해 보인다.

It **sounds** true.   그것은 사실처럼 들린다.

He **feels** better.   그는 더 나아진 것처럼 느낀다.

Good medicine **tastes** bitter.   좋은 약이 입에 쓰다. (쓴 맛이난다)

다음 형용사의 용법을 고르고 우리말로 옮겨 보자.

leg 다리
sunny 화창한

1 This is a sweet cake.　　　　　　　　(한정적 용법), 서술적 용법)

이것은　　　　달콤한　　　　케이크이다.
This cake is sweet.　　　　　　(한정적 용법, 서술적 용법)

이 케이크는　　　달콤하다　　　.

2 The boy is tall.　　　　　　　　(한정적 용법,　서술적 용법)

그 소년은　　　　　　　　.
He is a tall boy.　　　　　　　(한정적 용법,　서술적 용법)

그는　　　　　　　소년이다.

3 This rabbit is fast.　　　　　　(한정적 용법,　서술적 용법)

이 토끼는　　　　　　　.
This is a fast rabbit.　　　　　(한정적 용법,　서술적 용법)

이것은　　　　　　토끼이다.

4 She has long legs.　　　　　　(한정적 용법,　서술적 용법)

그녀는　　　　　　를 가지고 있다.
Her legs are long.　　　　　　(한정적 용법,　서술적 용법)

그녀의 다리는　　　　　　.

5 The weather is sunny.　　　　　(한정적 용법,　서술적 용법)

날씨가　　　　　　.
It is a sunny day today.　　　　(한정적 용법,　서술적 용법)

오늘은　　　　　　날이다.

2

다음 빈칸에 알맞은 형용사를 써 보자.

1	느린	*slow*	↔ 빠른	*fast*
2	추운		↔ 더운	
3	젊은		↔ 늙은	
4	슬픈		↔ 기쁜	
5	밝은		↔ 어두운	
6	강한		↔ 약한	
7	얕은		↔ 깊은	
8	키가 큰		↔ 키가 작은	
9	쉬운		↔ 어려운	
10	배고픈		↔ 배부른	
11	젖은		↔ 마른	
12	건강한		↔ 아픈	
13	낮은		↔ 높은	
14	가벼운		↔ 무거운	
15	행복한		↔ 불행한	

다음 빈칸에 알맞은 형용사를 써 보자.

1 작은   *small*   ↔ 큰   *big*

2 부지런한   ↔ 게으른

3 짧은   ↔ 긴

4 친절한   ↔ 불친절한

5 예쁜   ↔ 못생긴

6 어리석은   ↔ 영리한

7 가득 찬   ↔ 비어있는

8 깨끗한   ↔ 더러운

9 값비싼   ↔ 값싼

10 부유한   ↔ 가난한

11 바쁜   ↔ 한가한

12 열려 있는   ↔ 닫혀 있는

13 위험한   ↔ 안전한

14 뚱뚱한   ↔ 마른

15 좋은   ↔ 나쁜

4

다음 보기 A와 B에서 알맞은 말을 우리말에 알맞게 빈칸을 채워 보자.

A. sound   look   taste   smell   feel

B. crazy   worse   lonely   strong   sour   sleepy   sad
cold   good   salty   sweet   happy   bad

worse 더 나쁜
sleepy 졸리운
crazy 미친
strange 이상한
lonely 외로운

1 You   *look*   *worse*   .   너는 더 나빠 보인다.

You   .   너는 좋아 보인다.

You   .   너는 행복한 것처럼 보인다.

2 His song   .   그의 노래는 슬프게 들린다.

His music   .   그의 음악은 차갑게 들린다.

His words   .   그의 말은 미친 것처럼 들린다.

3 This sauce   .   이 소스는 짠 냄새가 난다.

The orange   .   그 오렌지는 신 냄새가 난다.

It   .   그것은 고린내가 난다. (나쁜 냄새가 난다)

4 The beef steak   .   그 비프스테이크는 좋은 맛이 난다.

This coffee   .   이 커피는 신 맛이 난다.

Onions   .   양파는 단 맛이 난다.

5 I   .   나는 졸립게 느껴진다.

I   .   나는 춥게 느껴진다.

I   .   나는 외롭게 느껴진다.

다음 주어진 단어를 이용하여 우리말에 알맞게 빈칸을 채워 보자.

partner 파트너
insect 곤충
diligent 부지런한, 근면한
deep 깊은
river 강
thief 도둑

1   *my*   *new*   *partner*

나의 새 파트너 (partner, new, my)

2

하나의 매우 긴 새 외투 (long, very, a, coat, new)

3

매우 작은 곤충들 (small, very, insects)

4

한 명의 부지런한 여자 (a, woman, diligent)

5

매우 깊은 강 (river, a, deep, very)

6

그의 위대한 그림들 (his, paintings, great)

7 '관사 + 부사 + 형상 +
신. 구 + 명사'의 순서이다.

7

한 명의 매우 강하고 젊은 남자 (young, very, man, strong, a)

8 '수량 + 대, 소 + 형상 +
명사'의 순서이다.

8

2개의 큰 갈색 잎들 (brown, leaves, two, big)

9

3명의 나쁜 도둑들 (three, thieves, bad)

10

하나의 매우 화창한 날 (day, very, a, sunny)

2

다음 우리말에 알맞게 빈칸을 채워 보자.

1 It is _his_ _red_ _tie_ .
그것은 그의 빨간 타이이다.

2 I am .
나는 좋은 축구 선수이다.

3 The are hers.
그 5벌의 짧고 빨간 치마는 그녀의 것이다.

4 This is .
이것은 매우 무거운 수박이다.

5 They are .
그들은 3명의 작고 예쁜 소녀들이다.

6 These are .
이것들은 높은 새 빌딩들이다.

7 He is .
그는 불쌍한 거지이다.

8 That man is .
저 사람은 매우 작고 뚱뚱한 농부이다.

9 Dogs are .
개들은 우리의 좋은 친구들이다.

10 My teacher has .
나의 선생님은 비싸고 오래된 괘종시계를 하나 가지고 계신다.

soccer player 축구선수
skirt 치마
beggar 거지
farmer 농부
clock 괘종시계

3 '수량 + 대, 소 + 형상 + 명사'의 순서이다.

5 '수량 + 대, 소 + 형상 + 명사'의 순서이다.

8 '관사 + 부사 + 대, 소 + 형상 + 명사'의 순서이다.

10 '관사 + 형상 + 신, 구 + 명사'의 순서이다.

우리말의 빈칸을 채우고, 우리말에 알맞게 빈칸을 채워 보자.

dirty 더러운
shallow 얕은
closed 닫은
dry 건조한
eggplant 가지
wonderful 놀라운
rich 부유한

1 나는 춥다. (= 이다 + 추운)

I *am* *cold* .

2 그의 바지는 더럽다. (= 이다 +)

His pants .

3 그 호수는 얕다. (= + 얕은)

The lake .

4 그 땅은 건조하다. (= + 건조한)

The land .

5 그 아이스크림 가게는 문을 닫았다. (= 이다 +)

The ice cream shop .

6 서울에는 폭풍이 친다. (= + 폭풍이 치는)

It in Seoul.

7 그는 아프다. (= 이다 +)

He .

8 이 가지들은 신선하다. (= 이다 +)

These eggplants .

9 이 세상은 놀랍다. (= 이다 +)

This world .

10 너는 부유하다. (= 이다 +)

You .

4

다음 우리말에 알맞게 빈칸을 채워 보자.

1 The oil price _____ *is* _____ *low* _____ .
기름 가격은 낮다.

2 His brother _____ .
그의 남동생은 게으르다.

3 Bananas _____ .
바나나는 노란색이다.

4 The window _____ .
그 창문은 크다.

5 Math and science _____ .
수학과 과학은 어렵다.

6 This well _____ .
이 우물은 말랐다. (비어 있다)

7 I _____ .
나는 배부르다.

8 Microwave ovens _____ .
전자 레인지들은 위험하다.

9 It _____ today.
오늘은 무덥다.

10 She _____ .
그녀는 한가하다.

oil 기름
price 가격
science 과학
Microwave oven 전자
레인지
dangerous 위험한
muggy 무더운
free 한가한

다음 두 문장의 뜻이 같도록 빈칸에 알맞은 말을 써 보자.

soldier 군인
front door 현관문

1 Those soldiers are strong.

= Those soldiers   *aren't*   *weak*   .

2 The beggar is happy.

= The beggar   .

3 This city isn't dangerous.

= This city   .

4 The ties are expensive.

= The ties   .

5 Jeff isn't diligent.

= Jeff   .

6 My hands are wet.

= My hands   .

7 The basketball players are tall.

= The basketball players   .

8 The snake is long.

= The snake   .

9 Airplanes aren't slow.

= Airplanes   .

10 The front door isn't open.

= The front door   .

6

다음 두 문장의 뜻이 같도록 빈칸에 알맞은 말을 써 보자.

schoolbag 책가방
shallow 얕은
healthy 건강한

1 My parents aren't young.

= My parents   *are*   *old*   .

2 Mary isn't hungry.

= Mary   .

3 Mr. Brown is rich.

= Mr. Brown   .

4 That well isn't shallow.

= That well   .

5 It's hot today.

= It   today.

6 Those buildings aren't low.

= Those buildings   .

7 These school bags aren't light.

= These school bags   .

8 She is healthy.

= She   .

9 It isn't dark here.

= It   here.

10 The girls are wise.

= The girls   .

우리말에 알맞게 빈칸을 채워 보자.

interesting 흥미로운
pale 창백한
better 더 나아진
comfortable 편안한
wonderful 놀라운
bitter 쓴
strange 낯선
bug 벌레
dead 죽은
awful 지독한

1 This bread *tastes* *bitter* .
이 빵은 쓴 맛이 난다.

2 The dish .
그 요리는 매운 냄새가 난다.

3 His speech .
그의 연설은 흥미있게 들린다.

4 She .
그녀는 창백해 보인다.

5 I with Jane.
나는 Jane과 함께 있으면 편안하게 느껴진다.

6 This coffee .
이 커피는 놀라운 맛이 난다.

7 This coat .
이 코트는 따뜻해 보인다.

8 His voice .
그의 목소리는 낯설게 들린다.

9 The bug .
그 벌레는 죽은 것처럼 보인다.

10 Your feet .
너의 발은 지독한 냄새가 난다.

우리말에 알맞게 빈칸을 채워 보자.

1 It doesn't *smell* *good* .

그것은 좋은 냄새가 나지 않는다.

2 You in the suit.

너는 그 정장을 입으니 멋져 보인다.

3 Your dress .

너의 드레스는 환상적으로 보인다.

4 The fish .

그 생선은 비린맛이 난다.

5 I .

나는 배고픈 것처럼 느낀다 (배가 고프다).

6 It .

그것은 딱딱하게 느껴진다.

7 She .

그녀는 추워 보인다.

8 My dad .

나의 아빠는 불안하게 보인다.

9 This Kimchi .

이 김치는 신 맛이 난다.

10 We on our feet.

우리는 우리의 발걸음이 가볍게 느껴진다.

nice 멋있는
fantastic 환상적인
fishy 비린내의
hard 딱딱한
nervous 신경이 예민한,
불안한

다음 밑줄 친 부분들 중에서 틀린 곳을 바르게 고쳐 써 보자.

excellent 탁월한
slim 날씬한

1   She is unkind a girl.
    an unkind girl

2   Those ants aren't bigs.

3   He is very a hungry beggar.

4   They foolish.

5   The roofs are blues.

6   This is a very old big table.

7   Tom is an very excellent pilot.

8   His farm large is.

9   Mary and Judy are slim very dancers.

10 Those are new seven televisions.

11 These turtles are greens.

12 They feel merrily.

13 This coffee tastes strongly.

14 His cousins are boys little.

2

다음 밑줄 친 부분들 중에서 틀린 곳을 바르게 고쳐 써 보자.

empty 비어있는
blanket 담요
stove 난로
skinny 마른
terrible 끔찍한
radish 무우

1 Starcraft <u>is</u> <u>very exciting a game</u>.
   a very exciting game

2 <u>The</u> boxes <u>empty</u>.

3 There <u>are</u> <u>comfortable very</u> running shoes.

4 These <u>blankets</u> are <u>wets</u>.

5 Sally and Liz <u>are</u> her <u>lovely small</u> children.

6 The chocolate <u>smells</u> <u>sweetly</u>.

7 That <u>is</u> <u>very a hot stove</u>.

8 His voice <u>sounds</u> <u>deeply</u>.

9 <u>Those</u> bears are <u>bigs</u>.

10 Mr. Brown and Mr. Smith <u>are</u> <u>old rich</u> people.

11 The idea <u>sounds</u> <u>terriblely</u>.

12 You <u>are</u> <u>kind very</u>.

13 <u>Her mom</u> looks <u>happily</u>.

14 This radish <u>tastes</u> <u>bitterly</u>.

01 다음 중 반대말끼리 짝지어지지 <u>않은</u> 것은?

① old - young   ② sad - glad
③ fast - big   ④ dry - wet
⑤ hot - cold

02 다음 (   ) 안의 단어가 순서에 맞게 배열된 것은?

02

sport 운동

Soccer is (exciting, a, sport, very)

① very an exciting sport
② an exciting sport very
③ a very exciting sport
④ very exciting a sport
⑤ exciting a very sport

03 다음 문장을 복수형으로 바르게 바꿔 쓴 것은?

That sweater is warm.

① That sweaters is warm.
② Those sweater are warm.
③ Those sweaters is warm.
④ Those sweaters are warms.
⑤ Those sweaters are warm.

O4 다음 문장 중 바른 것은?

① She is my a good teacher.
② These are long two snakes.
③ You are very a happy girl.
④ They are three big watermelons.
⑤ That is new his car.

정답 및 해설 p.12

O5 다음 명사들을 |보기|와 같이 바꿔 쓰시오.

O5

mug 잔에 갇힌 것처럼 답답하다는 느낌으로 muggy는 후덥지근하다는 것을 나타내는 형용사이다.

| 보기 |　sun 해 → sunny 햇볕이 비치는

a. rain 비 　　　→ ＿＿＿＿＿＿＿＿ 비가 오는

b. cloud 구름 　→ ＿＿＿＿＿＿＿＿ 구름 낀

c. wind 바람 　→ ＿＿＿＿＿＿＿＿ 바람이 부는

d. snow 눈 　　→ ＿＿＿＿＿＿＿＿ 눈이 오는

e. storm 폭풍 　→ ＿＿＿＿＿＿＿＿ 폭풍이 치는

f. fog 안개 　　→ ＿＿＿＿＿＿＿＿ 안개 낀

g. mug 머그잔 →＿＿＿＿＿＿＿＿ 후덥지근한

06 다음 문장의 의미와 같도록 빈칸에 알맞은 형용사를 쓰시오.

Maria is short and skinny.

= Maria isn't _____ and _____.

07 다음 우리말에 맞도록 ( ) 안의 단어를 바르게 배열하여 문장을 쓰시오.

나의 아버지는 매우 유명한 나이 든 의사이시다.

(old, doctor, very, my, father, a, famous, is)

→ _____

08 다음은 반대의 뜻을 가진 형용사를 적은 것이다. ( ) 안에 공통으로 들어갈 수 있는 철자를 쓰시오.

happy	↔	( ) happy
kind	↔	( ) kind
wise	↔	( ) wise
able	↔	( ) able

09 다음 문장 중 어법상 옳지 <u>않는</u> 것은?

① He looks happy.
② He looks sad.
③ He looks lovely.
④ He looks sick.
⑤ He looks very cutely.

09

cutely 귀엽게

감각동사+형용사

10 다음 중 밑줄 친 형용사의 쓰임이 <u>다른</u> 것은?

① It is a <u>long</u> river.
② They are <u>kind</u> women.
③ She has a <u>nice</u> coat.
④ Tom is <u>happy</u>.
⑤ We eat <u>fresh</u> oranges.

10

형용사는 명사를 꾸며
주거나 주어를 설명해
주는 역할을 한다.

정답 및 해설 **P.12**

다음 우리말에 알맞게 빈칸을 채워 보자.

1 Judy _____.

Judy는 불쌍하다.

2 That cat _____. awful 지독한

저 고양이는 지독한 냄새가 난다.

3 I _____. better 더 좋은

나는 더 좋아진 느낌이다.

4 You have _____ dogs.

너는 세 마리의 작고 사랑스러운 개를 가지고 있다.

5 This ship _____.

이 배는 멋지게 보인다.

6 There are _____ questions in this exam.

이 시험에는 어려운 문제가 3개가 있다.

7 It _____ and _____ today.

오늘은 바람이 불고 안개가 낀 날이다.

8 I know _____ museum.

나는 크고 오래된 박물관을 하나 알고 있다.

9 Lemons _____.

레몬들은 신 맛이 난다.

10 Students want _____ games.

학생들은 흥미롭고 새로운 게임들을 원한다.

Unit 06

some, any와 many, much, a lot of

some과 any는 '몇몇의, 약간의'라는 뜻으로 많지 않은 수를 나타내며, many, much, a lot of 은 '많은' 이라는 뜻을 가진다.

Unit 06

some, any와 many, much, a lot of

① some과 any

'몇몇의, 약간의'라는 뜻으로 많지 않은 수를 나타낸다.

① some이나 any 뒤에 오는 셀 수 있는 명사는 복수 형태로 온다.

| some, any | 약간의 | +복수명사 |

ex. I have **some** apples. 나는 몇 개의 사과를 가지고 있다.
~~I have some apple.~~

I don't have **any** books. 나는 몇 권의 책도 가지고 있지 않다.
~~I don't have any book.~~

② some이나 any 뒤에 오는 셀 수 없는 명사는 복수형으로 올 수 없다.

ex. I drink some milk. 나는 약간의 우유를 마신다.
~~I drink some milks.~~

> **Tip!** some, any가 '어떤, 어느'의 뜻을 나타낼 때는 뒤에 단수/셀 수 있는 명사가 올 수 있다.
> ex. Take any book you need. 필요한 어떤 책이든 가져가.

* 본 unit에서는 some, any가 '몇몇의, 약간의' 뜻으로 쓰이는 경우만 다루기로 한다.

③ 보통 긍정문에서는 some, 부정문과 의문문에서는 any를 쓴다. 단 제안, 부탁의 경우는 의문문일지라도 some을 사용한다.

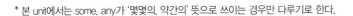
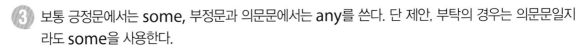

		some	any
긍정문		I have **some** books. 나는 몇 권의 책을 가지고 있다.	–
부정문		–	I don't have **any** books. 나는 몇 권의 책도 가지고 있지 않다.
의문문	제안	Would you like **some** tea? 차 좀 드시겠어요?	Do you have **any** books? 너는 몇 권의 책을 가지고 있니?
	부탁	Can I have **some** soup? 내가 수프를 좀 먹어도 되겠니?	

Tip! **Do you have some money?**와 **Do you have any money?**의 차이

보통 의문문에서는 any를 사용하지만 이미 알고 있거나 그렇다고 생각할 때는 some을 사용한다.

ex. Do you have some money? 너 돈 좀 있지?

그러나 돈이 있는지 없는지 확실히 모르는 경우는 보통 의문문에서 처럼 any를 사용한다

ex. Do you have any money? 너 돈 좀 가진거 있니?

2 many, much, a lot of

① '많은'의 뜻으로 쓰이고 많은 수나 양을 나타내며, 뒤에 오는 셀 수 있는 명사는 복수 형태가 온다.

many, a lot of	+ 셀 수 **있는** 명사 (복수)
much, a lot of	+ 셀 수 **없는** 명사

ex. There are a lot of apples in the box. 상자에는 많은 사과가 있다.

There isn't much rain in July. 7월에는 많은 비가 내리지 않는다.

② **many**와 **a lot of**는 긍정문, 부정문, 의문문 모두에 사용할 수 있지만 **much**는 부정문, 의문문에 사용하고 긍정문에는 사용하지 않는다. 긍정문에서는 **much** 대신 **a lot of**를 사용한다.

	긍정문	부정문	의문문
many	There are many pens.	I don't have many pens.	How many pens are there?
much	I buy much salt.	I don't buy much salt.	Do you buy much salt?
a lot of	There are a lot of books. I buy a lot of salt.	I don't have a lot of pens. I don't buy a lot of salt.	Do you have a lot of pens? Do you buy a lot of salt?

단, **much**가 **very, too, so**와 함께 오는 경우 긍정문에서도 **much**를 사용한다.

ex. She drinks **too much** water a day. 그녀는 하루에 너무 많은 물을 마신다.

Tip! ❶ 어법상 many는 긍정문에 사용할 수 있으나 보통 잘 쓰지 않는다. 따라서 보통 명사의 종류와 상관없이 긍정문에서는 a lot of를 쓴다고 생각하면 된다.

❷ many, much는 very, too, so와 함께 오는 경우에는 a lot of로 바꿔 쓸 수 없다.

ex. too many books ~~too a lot of books~~

다음 (   ) 안에서 알맞은 말을 골라 동그라미 해 보자.

ruler 자
sunflower 해바라기
on one's way home
집에 오는 길에
palace 궁전
flour 밀가루

1 They have some (candy, (candies)).

2 Does Tom cut any (tree, trees)?

3 Would you buy some (butter, butters) on your way home?

4 He doesn't have any (rulers, ruler).

5 There are some (sunflower, sunflowers) in this garden.

6 I sometimes eat some (cheeses, cheese).

7 He doesn't see (some, any) palaces.

다음 (   ) 안에서 알맞은 말을 골라 동그라미 해 보자.

1 She puts (some, any) flour in a jar.

2 Does John carry (some, any) orange boxes?

3 He asks (some, any) questions.

4 She doesn't kill (some, any) butterflies.

5 There are (some, any) hens in this farm.

6 We don't have (some, any) tomatoes.

7 Can I have (some, any) candies?

2

다음 ( ) 안에서 알맞은 말을 골라 동그라미 해 보자.

1 I don't drink (many, (much)) water in winter.

2 There aren't (many, much) foxes in the forest.

3 I don't have (many, much) milk.

4 She doesn't count (many, much) sheep.

5 Does he draw (many, much) beautiful pictures?

6 My brother doesn't eat (many, much) carrots.

7 There aren't (many, much) ants under the tree.

8 Do you make (many, much) flowers with paper?

9 I don't want (many, much) honey.

10 Does Jack repair (many, much) cars?

11 The mouse doesn't eat (many, much) cheese.

12 Mrs. Brown doesn't wear (many, much) accessories.

13 Does he bring (many, much) flower pots?

14 She doesn't use (many, much) erasers.

15 There isn't (many, much) jam in the bottle.

under ~아래에
with paper 종이를 가지고
accessory 장신구
flower pot 화분

다음 ( ) 안에서 알맞은 말을 골라 동그라미 해 보자. (2가지 가능)

gun 총
change 변화
ticket 표

1 She opens (many, much, a lot of) bottles of water.

2 The rabbit doesn't have (many, much, a lot of) carrots.

3 Does he have (many, much, a lot of) guns?

4 They don't buy (many, much, a lot of) flour.

5 He wants (many, much, a lot of) money.

6 I get (many, much, a lot of) information.

7 John has too (many, much, a lot of) dogs.

8 My daughter makes (many, much, a lot of) changes.

9 Thank you very (many, much, a lot of).

10 She needs (many, much, a lot of) help.

11 Does she have (many, much, a lot of) tickets?

12 Do you read (many, much, a lot of) interesting books?

13 He gives (many, much, a lot of) flowers to Jill.

14 He saves (many, much, a lot of) rice.

15 She sends me (many, much, a lot of) samples.

4

다음 (   ) 안에서 알맞은 말을 골라 동그라미 해 보자. (2가지 가능)

1 You have (many, much, a lot of) ice cream.

2 She drinks (many, much, a lot of) milk.

3 Matt and his wife buy (many, much, a lot of) bananas.

4 He spends (many, much, a lot of) time for shopping.

5 Does John grill (many, much, a lot of) fish?

6 The washing machine needs (many, much, a lot of) water.

7 They found so (many, much, a lot of) gold in the cave.

8 Are there (many, much, a lot of) people in Paris?

9 These cars don't need (many, much, a lot of) oil.

10 His mother feels too (many, much, a lot of) pain.

11 I try to get (many, much, a lot of) scores.

12 Do they eat (many, much, a lot of) cookies a day?

13 Jim works (many, much, a lot of) time.

14 Does he eat (many, much, a lot of) meat everyday?

15 I get (many, much, a lot of) food.

grill 굽다
stew 국, 찌개
washing machine 세탁기
found (find의 과거) 찾았다
cave 동굴
pain 통증
snack 간식

다음 빈칸에 some이나 any 중에서 알맞은 것을 골라 써 넣어 보자.

coupon 쿠폰
collect 모으다, 수집하다
foreign 외국의
carrot 당근
pine tree 소나무
number 숫자
word 단어
accessory 장식품

1 I don't save ___*any*___ coupons.

2 Do you collect ___ data?

3 He meets ___ foreign friends.

4 We don't know ___ people in Canada.

5 Does John sell ___ carrots?

6 She doesn't write ___ letters.

7 We bring ___ pine trees.

8 I don't remember ___ phone numbers.

9 Does he drink ___ Coke?

10 Would you lend me ___ money?

11 They don't carry ___ spoons.

12 Are there ___ forks on the table?

13 There are ___ bears in the zoo.

14 She doesn't wear ___ bracelets.

15 Can I take ___ comic books?

2

다음 문장을 지시대로 바꿔 보자.

1 Mr. Kim keeps some pigs.

의문문   *Does Mr. Kim keep any pigs?*

2 She washes some strawberries.

부정문

3 I write some novels.

부정문

4 Her mother helps some poor people.

의문문

5 He teaches some smart students.

의문문

6 She slices some cheese off.

부정문

7 You visit some places in Turkey.

의문문

8 There are some holidays in this month.

부정문

9 You need some help now.

의문문

10 It has some dangers.

부정문

novel 소설
poor 가난한
smart 똑똑한
slice ~ off 얇게 저미다
place 장소
Turkey 터키
month 달, 월
danger 위험

＊ some이 의문문, 부정문
  에서는 any로 바뀐다.

다음 빈칸에 many, much, a lot of 중에서 알맞은 것을 골라 써 넣어 보자. (2가지 가능)

pour 붓다
hole 구멍
December 12월
museum 박물관
schedule 스케줄을 짜다
overtime 초과 근무
flour 밀가루
yogurt 요구르트

1 I sing *many, a lot of* songs.

2 He doesn't pour   oil into the hole.

3 We look after   children.

4 Do you eat   vegetable every morning?

5   people love her.

6 John doesn't bring   story books.

7 There are too   colors in this picture.

8 We have   snow in December.

9 There are   museums in New York.

10 He schedules   overtime.

11 She doesn't have too   homework.

12 Jane doesn't want   flour.

13 The woman gets   salt every year.

14 They build   houses.

15 Does your grandmother make   yogurt?

4

다음 빈칸에 many, much, a lot of 중에서 알맞은 것을 골라 써 넣어 보자. (2가지 가능)

1 There isn't _much, a lot of_ oxygen in this tank.

2 Does she have   friends in her school?

3 We don't travel   countries in the world.

4 There is   butter in the refrigerator.

5 Do you have   hard work?

6 I need   pens for the test.

7 She has so   salad at every meal.

8 Now, it needs too   air.

9 I make   money.

10 Does he see   fans from Japan?

11 I don't eat   melons in a day.

12 He keeps too   dogs.

13 We buy   food from the grocery store.

14 Tom sweeps out   fallen leaves in the backyard.

15 There are so   women at the mall.

oxygen 산소
tank 탱크, 통
meal 끼니
air 공기
fan 팬
Japan 일본
grocery store 식료품가게
sweep 쓸다
fallen leaf 낙엽
backyard 뒤뜰

다음 밑줄 친 부분들 중에서 틀린 곳을 바르게 고쳐 써 보자.

borrow 빌리다
difficult 어려운
problem 문제
free sample 견본 제품
question 질문
bridge 다리
clothing store 옷가게
green onion 파
on your way home 집에 오
는 길에
rule 규칙
repeat 반복하다

* some, any + 셀 수 있는
복수명사, 셀 수 없는 단수
명사

1 I call <u>some</u> <u>student</u>.
   students

2 Are there <u>some</u> English <u>speakers</u> here?

3 Does he meet <u>some</u> soccer <u>players</u>?

4 My father has <u>any</u> wonderful <u>paintings</u>.

5 Does Inho borrow <u>some</u> <u>notebooks</u>?

6 Can I have some <u>sugars</u> for my <u>coffee</u>?

7 They have <u>any</u> difficult <u>problems</u>.

8 He is picking up <u>some</u> free <u>sample</u>.

9 Do you make <u>some</u> <u>money</u> every month?

10 <u>Some</u> <u>bridge</u> in this city are very strong.

11 There aren't <u>some</u> clothing <u>stores</u> around here.

12 Would you type <u>any</u> <u>letters</u> for me?

13 They make <u>any</u> <u>rules</u> for their team.

14 Do you need <u>some</u> <u>help</u>?

15 We don't use <u>any</u> <u>word</u>.

2

다음 밑줄 친 부분들 중에서 틀린 곳을 바르게 고쳐 써 보자.

1 There isn't <u>many</u> <u>money</u> in my pocket.
  a lot of, much

2 James hits <u>many</u> <u>ball</u>.

3 There is <u>many</u> <u>information</u> in the file.

4 Tom has <u>much</u> <u>keys</u> in the drawer.

5 There is <u>Much</u> <u>gas</u> under the ground.

6 I think <u>about</u> it many <u>time</u>.

7 It has <u>a lot of</u> <u>funs</u>.

8 <u>Many</u> <u>child</u> swim in the pool.

9 Do your parents want <u>many</u> <u>white wine</u>?

10 My father writes <u>much</u> <u>novels</u>.

11 Ann fries <u>much</u> <u>eggs</u>.

12 He doesn't mix <u>many</u> <u>flour</u>.

13 <u>Many</u> <u>tiger</u> live in Africa.

14 <u>Much</u> <u>rice</u> is in this plastic bag.

15 Too <u>many</u> <u>leaf</u> fall down.

key 열쇠
drawer 서랍
ground 땅
time 시간/~번
wine 포도주
novel 소설
Africa 아프리카

01 다음 중 빈칸에 들어갈 말로 알맞지 <u>않은</u> 것은?

> I have some _____.

① bananas ② carrots
③ waters ④ notebooks
⑤ pencils

02 다음 중 빈칸에 any가 들어갈 수 있는 문장은?

① She eats _____ apple pies.
② I don't have _____ tickets.
③ Mr. Brown writes _____ letters.
④ Mom wants _____ salt.
⑤ He buys _____ CDs.

03 다음 문장을 부정문으로 바르게 바꿔 쓴 것은?

03
storybook 이야기책

> He has some storybooks in his room.

① He doesn't have some storybook in his room.
② He doesn't has some storybooks in his room.
③ He don't have any storybook in his room.
④ He doesn't has some storybooks in his room.
⑤ He doesn't have any storybooks in his room.

04 다음 빈칸에 들어갈 말이 순서대로 바르게 짝지어진 것을 고르시오.

> • Can I have _____ cookies?
>
> • Does he make _____ chairs?
>
> • There aren't _____ teachers in the party.

① some - any - any
② any - some - some
③ some - any - some
④ some - some - any
⑤ any - any - some

05 틀린 곳을 찾아 바르게 고쳐 보시오.

> Much babies sleep well.

_____ ⇨ _____

06 다음 빈칸에 공통으로 들어갈 수 있는 말을 고르시오.

> · Would you like _____ tea?
>
> · Can you bring _____ paper?

① much   ② all

③ some   ④ any

⑤ many

07 같은 뜻이 되도록 빈칸을 채워 보시오.

> I buy many candies.
>
> = I buy _____ candies.

08 다음 우리말을 영어로 바르게 옮긴 것 두 가지는?

> 그 병에는 많은 주스가 있니?

① Is there many juice in the bottle?

② Are there much juice in the bottle?

③ Is there much juice in the bottle?

④ Are therea lot of juice in the bottle?

⑤ Is there a lot of juice in the bottle?

09 다음 문장에서 <u>틀린</u> 부분을 찾아 바르게 고쳐 쓰시오.

> She uses too a lot of sugar in her food.

_____ ⇨ _____

10 다음 빈칸에 공통으로 들어갈 말로 알맞은 것은?

> · She eats _____ cookies.
>
> · He drinks _____ soda.

① many
② much
③ a lot of
④ lot
⑤ very

Quiz!

다음 빈칸에 some과 any 중에서 알맞은 것을 골라 써 넣어 보자.

1 I eat   candies.

2 He doesn't kill   animals.   kill 죽이다

3 Jane buys   potatoes.

4 Can I have   grape juice?   grape 포도

5 Does the woman sell   sweaters?   sweater 스웨터

6 We order   hamburgers.

7 Do you have   tennis balls?

다음 빈칸에 many, much, a lot of 중에서 알맞은 것을 골라 써 넣어 보자. (2가지 가능)

1   paintings are in the museum.

많은 그림이 박물관에 있다.

2 Do you send   flowers to her?

너는 그녀에게 많은 꽃을 보내니?

3 Mary cleans   bedrooms in the hotel.

Mary는 그 호텔에 있는 많은 방들을 청소한다.

4 My father doesn't need   time for the work.

나의 아버지는 그 일을 하시는 데 많은 시간이 필요치 않다.

5 I buy   cheese.

나는 많은 치즈를 산다.

6 Why do you waste so   money?   waste 낭비하다

너는 왜 그렇게 많은 돈을 낭비하니?

7 He doesn't wear   rings.

그는 많은 반지를 끼지 않는다.

Unit 07

부사

동사, 형용사, 다른 부사 등을 꾸며 주는 말로서
우리말로 「～하게」라는 뜻이 많다.
위치는 형용사 앞이나 주로 문장의
뒤에 오게 되나, 강조할 때는
문장 앞에 오기도 한다.

부사

부사란?

동사, 형용사, 다른 부사 등을 꾸며 주는 말로서 우리말로 「~하게」라는 뜻이 많다.

1 쓰임

▶ 형용사를 꾸며 주는 경우

ex. She is a very smart girl. 그녀는 매우 영리한 소녀이다.
부사 　　형용사 　명사

▶ 동사를 꾸며 주는 경우

ex. He runs fast. 그는 빠르게 달린다.
동사 　부사

▶ 다른 부사를 꾸며 주는 경우

ex. He runs very fast. 그는 매우 빠르게 달린다.
부사 　부사

2 형태

대부분의 부사는 형용사에 ly를 붙여 만듭니다.
(단, '자음 + y'로 끝나는 형용사는 y를 i로 바꾸고 ly를 붙여 줍니다.)

형용사 + ly = 부사

bad 나쁜, 못된		badly 나쁘게(심하게), 못되게
beautiful 아름다운		beautifully 아름답게
careful 조심스러운		carefully 조심스럽게
quick 빠른	+ ly	quickly 빠르게
safe 안전한		safely 안전하게
loud 시끄러운		loud, loudly 시끄럽게
slow 느린		slow, slowly 느리게
easy 쉬운		easily 쉽게
angry 화가난	y를 지우고 + ily	angrily 화가 나서
heavy 무거운		heavily 무겁게, 힘겹게
pretty 예쁜		prettily 예쁘게

ex. The child crosses the street **safely**. 그 어린이는 안전하게 길을 건넌다.

▶ 형용사와 부사의 형태가 같은 것

early 이른	**early** 이르게
fast 빠른	**fast** 빠르게
hard 열심히 노력하는	**hard** 열심히
high 높은	**high** 높게
late 늦은	**late** 늦게

> **Tip!** '꾸며준다(수식하다)'는 두 단어를 이어서 말할 때 자연스러우면 앞에 있는 단어가 뒤에 있는 단어를 꾸며주는 것이다.
> *ex.* 매우 영리한 소녀
>   매우 소녀

ex. The **early** bird catches the worm.   일찍 일어나는 새가 벌레를 잡는다.
   She always arrives **early**.   그녀는 항상 일찍 도착한다.

▶ 형용사와 부사의 형태가 전혀 다른 것

good 좋은	well 잘

> **Tip!** 「매우」라는 뜻을 가진 부사로는 very, so, quite가 있고, 「너무」라는 부정적 의미를 가진 부사로 too가 있다.

ex. She is a **good** doctor.   그녀는 좋은 의사이다. (형용사)
   She swims **well**.   그녀는 수영을 잘 한다. (부사)

3 빈도 부사

▶ 의미 : 횟수를 나타내는 부사

always	항상	rarely	드물게, 좀처럼 ~않다
often	자주, 종종	seldom	좀처럼 ~않다
usually	보통	hardly	거의 ~않다
sometimes	가끔, 때때로	never	결코 ~않다

> **Tip!** 때에 따라서는 강조하기 위하여 빈도부사가 문장의 앞, 뒤에 오기도 한다.

▶ 위치 : 주로 be동사, 조동사 뒤에, 일반동사 앞에 온다.

> be동사, 조동사 + 빈도부사 + 일반동사

ex. I am **always** happy.   나는 항상 행복하다.
      be동사
   I will **always** study English.   나는 항상 영어 공부를 할 것이다.
      조동사
   I **sometimes** study English.   나는 가끔 영어 공부를 한다.
             일반동사

▶ rarely, seldom, hardly, never는 이미 부정의 의미가 포함되어 있으므로 부정문에는 쓸 수 없다.

ex. He **rarely** studies English.   그는 영어를 거의 공부하지 않는다.
   ~~He doesn't rarely study English.~~

기초다지기 1

다음 빈칸에 알맞은 형용사나 부사를 써 보자.

1	*fast*	빠른 →	**fast**	빠르게
2		안전한 →	**safely**	안전하게
3	late	늦은 →		늦게
4	easy	쉬운 →		쉽게
5		위험한 →	**dangerously**	위험하게
6	high	높은 →		높게
7	quick	빠른 →		빠르게
8		무거운 →	**heavily**	무겁게, 힘겹게
9	loud	시끄러운 →		시끄럽게
10	hard	열심히 하는 →		열심히
11	slow	느린 →		느리게
12		훌륭한 →	**well**	잘
13	careful	조심스러운 →		조심스럽게
14	angry	화난 →		화가 나서
15		아름다운 →	**beautifully**	아름답게

2

다음 빈칸에 알맞은 빈도 부사 또는 우리말 뜻을 써 보자.

1	가끔, 때때로	*sometimes*
2	거의 ~ 않다	
3		never
4	항상	
5	자주, 종종	
6	결코 ~ 않다	
7	가끔	
8		rarely, seldom
9	보통	
10		always
11		usually
12	드물게, 좀처럼 ~ 않다	
13		often
14		hardly

밑줄 친 단어가 꾸며주는 말에 동그라미 한 후 형용사인지 부사인지 고르고
우리말로 옮겨 보자.

building 건물
leave 떠나다
stay up 안자다 (깨어있다)
sink 가라앉다

1 The airplane (flies) high.　　　　　　(형용사, (부사))

⇨ 그 비행기는　　　　높게 날아간다　　　.

It is a high building.　　　　　　(형용사 , 부사)

⇨ 그것은　　　　　　　　　　.

2 He works hard everyday.　　　　　　(형용사, 부사)

⇨ 그는 매일　　　　　　　　　.

We have a hard time.　　　　　　(형용사, 부사)

⇨ 우리는　　　　　　　　　.

3 Tom leaves early everyday.　　　　　　(형용사, 부사)

⇨ Tom은 매일　　　　　　　　.

They meet in the early winter.　　　　　　(형용사, 부사)

⇨ 그들은　　　　　　　　　.

4 They have late dinner.　　　　　　(형용사, 부사)

⇨ 그들은　　　　　　　　　.

She stays up late.　　　　　　(형용사, 부사)

⇨ 그녀는　　　　　　　　　.

5 This dish is fast and easy.　　　　　　(형용사, 부사)

⇨ 이 요리는　　　　　　　　.

The boat is sinking fast.　　　　　　(형용사, 부사)

⇨ 그 보트는　　　　　　　　.

4

다음 ( ) 안에서 알맞은 말을 골라 동그라미 해 보자. (2가지 가능)

1 He runs (fast, fastly).

2 Jenny acts very (good, well).

3 She smiles (happy, happily).

4 She falls asleep (easy, easily).

5 It is a (perfect, perfectly) game.

6 She is a (kind, kindly) old lady.

7 My father is (angry, angrily).

8 I win the game (perfect, perfectly).

9 The earthworm moves (slow, slowly)

10 We are (good, well) tellers.

11 He finds her office (easy, easily).

12 The child goes to bed (early, earlily).

13 Bill is (bad, badly) at science.

14 Poison gas is (dangerous, dangerously).

15 I move to him (quick, quickly).

act 연기하다
fall asleep 잠들다
win 이기다
earthworm 지렁이
teller 은행창구직원
science 과학
poison gas 독가스

다음 ( ) 안에서 알맞은 말을 골라 동그라미 해 보자. (2가지 가능)

painting 그림
in life 인생에서
problem 문제
peach 복숭아
soldier 군인
shout 소리지르다
listen 듣다
fire 불
bill 계산서

1 She goes to work (early, earily).

2 We have (heavy, heavily) rain in summer.

3 You are so (loud, loudly).

4 He started painting (late, lately) in life.

5 The math problem is (easy, easily).

6 These peaches are (very, well) fresh.

7 The child crosses the street (safe, safely).

8 The soldier shouts (angry, angrily).

9 Listen (careful, carefully).

10 Jane mixes (very, well).

11 Fire is very (dangerous, dangerously).

12 He teaches me very (kind, kindly).

13 I draw him (perfect, perfectly).

14 She is (good, well) at sports.

15 The bill is too (high, highly).

6

다음 ( ) 안에 주어진 빈도부사의 위치로 주로 쓰이는 곳을 골라 보자.

1 My ① mom ②cooks ③ Bulgogi. (sometimes)

2 I ① meet ② him ③ with ④ Matt ⑤ . (seldom)

3 He ① is ② rich. (never)

4 My ① parents ② walk ③ to ④ the ⑤ market. (often)

5 They ① will ② go ③ to ④ church ⑤ on Sundays. (always)

6 He ① sings ② a ③ song. (rarely)

7 The student ① is ② late ③ for ④ meeting. (usually)

8 Tom ① hangs ② out ③ with ④ his friend. (sometimes)

9 Mary ① speaks ② Chinese. (seldom)

10 She ① will ② play ③ the ④ violin. (never)

11 His ① sister ② washes ③ the ④ dishes. (rarely)

12 Students ① stay ② up ③ late ④ studying. (usually)

13 Jane ① wears ② the ③ red ④ sweater. (often)

14 ①I ② go ③ to ④ my ⑤ house ⑥ for ⑦ lunch. (hardly)

15 She ① is ② diligent. (always)

hang out (~에서) 많은 시간을 보내다
stay up late studying 밤 늦게까지 공부하다

주어진 단어를 알맞은 형태로 바꿔 빈칸을 채워 보자.

final exam 기말고사
bite 물다
score a goal 골을 넣다
aim 목표로 삼다
motorcycle 오토바이
medicine 약
work 작용하다
quiet 조용한
quite 꽤, 상당히

1 My friend draws roses _beautifully_ . (beautiful)

2 I take the final exam . (easy)

3 Be . The dog can bite you. (careful)

4 We had a time. (nice)

5 He always drives . (dangerous)

6 The water in this town is not . (safe)

7 Tom scores a goal in the soccer game. (perfect)

8 She talks to her student . (soft)

9 Learning English is . (hard)

10 Aim ! We can do it! (high)

11 His voice is too . (loud)

12 He rides a motorcycle very . (fast)

13 She closes the window . (quiet)

14 This medicine works quite . (good)

15 She is a teacher at school. (good)

2

주어진 단어를 알맞은 형태로 바꿔 빈칸을 채워 보자.

1 The car goes very *slow, slowly* but very *nicely* ! (slow, nice)

2 I study _____ for my future. (hard)

3 Your kite is small and _____ . (quick)

4 He hurts his foot _____ . (bad)

5 There are two _____ questions. (difficult)

6 The fire fighters put out the fire _____ . (safe)

7 Your design is _____ . (perfect)

8 You must think _____ and act. (careful)

9 _____ food isn't good for health. (fast)

10 I have lunch in the _____ afternoon. (late)

11 She perms the man's hair very _____ . (nice)

12 It rains _____ every year. (heavy)

13 I sleep _____ and get up _____ . (early, late)

14 I am _____ about you. Because you are always _____ . (angry, late)

15 Jane bakes some _____ bread. (hard)

future 미래
question 질문
put out 끄다
design 디자인
must think 생각해야만 한다
act 행동하다
perm 파마하다
because 왜냐하면

꼭꼭 다지기 **3**

주어진 말을 사용하여 다음 문장을 완성해 보자.

miss 그리워하다
clothes 옷
credit card 신용 카드
fresh 신선한

1 I *always* *drink* some tomato juice.
(drink, always)

2 She her old friend.
(miss, sometimes)

3 Peter busy.
(be, usually)

4 I will my clothes.
(change, often)

5 My father books.
(read, hardly)

6 Susan her credit card.
(use, usually)

7 Jenny can him.
(see, rarely)

8 We skiing.
(enjoy, sometimes)

9 The watermelon fresh.
(be, never)

10 The child baseball with Tom.
(play, seldom)

7 can '~ 할 수 있다'의 뜻을 지닌 조동사

4

두 문장 중에서 옳은 것을 골라 동그라미 해 보자.

1 Jane seldom feeds her bird.   ○
    Jane rarely doesn't feed her bird.

2 I don't hardly tidy up my room.
    I never tide up my room.

3 He never tells a lie.
    He doesn't seldom tell a lie.

4 We don't rarely play a computer game.
    We hardly play a computer game.

feed 먹이를 주다
tidy up 정리하다
tell a lie 거짓말하다
wrong 틀린
Mt. Everest 에베레스트 산
be covered with ~로 덮여
있다

보기에서 질문에 해당하는 것을 골라 써 보자.

| 보기 | a. I am happy.
      b. He works ten hours a day.
      c. She will invite John.
      d. You don't have sweet cookies after meals.
      e. Mom is not wrong.
      f. She doesn't drink cold water.
      g. Mt. Everest is covered with snow.
      h. They don't go camping with Jack.
      i. He doesn't read a newspaper.
      j. I don't call Tom at night.

1 rarely, seldom, hardly, never를 쓸 수 없는 문장을 고르면?

다음 밑줄 친 부분들 중에서 틀린 곳을 바르게 고쳐 써 보자.

on foot 걸어서
weep 울다, 흐느끼다
explain 설명하다
run away 도망치다
kick hard 냅다 걸어차다

1 She <u>goes often</u> to the market <u>on foot</u>.
　　often goes

2 A girl <u>is</u> weeping <u>sad</u>.

3 Jack <u>arrives</u> at home <u>lately</u>.

4 <u>My</u> teacher <u>kindly explains</u>.

5 The classroom <u>often is</u> <u>noisy</u>.

6 <u>He</u> is an <u>honestly</u> man.

7 The boys <u>run away</u> <u>quick</u>.

8 He <u>seldom doesn't</u> <u>wears</u> socks.

9 David <u>always can meet</u> his parents.

10 Ann <u>wakes sometimes</u> <u>up</u> at 6.

11 The price is <u>too</u> <u>highly</u>.

12 The baby <u>doesn't</u> never <u>smiles</u>.

13 Tommy <u>doesn't</u> rarely <u>cleans</u> his desk.

14 He <u>kicks</u> <u>hardly</u>.

15 The boys <u>sometimes are</u> foolish.

다음 밑줄 친 부분들 중에서 틀린 곳을 바르게 고쳐 써 보자.

1 She doesn't <u>never</u> <u>talk with</u> Mr. Park.
     ✕

2 He <u>often is</u> <u>late</u> for the meeting.

3 These girls are <u>real</u> <u>beautiful</u>.

4 I type <u>very</u> <u>fastly</u>.

5 He <u>works never</u> hard at school.

6 I <u>play</u> tennis and golf <u>good</u>.

7 She <u>tells</u> her secret to others <u>easy</u>.

8 Judy is a <u>good</u> player. She <u>practices always</u> every day.

9 A subway <u>usually is</u> faster <u>than</u> a car.

10 Your children are <u>so</u> <u>cutely</u>.

11 Onions burn <u>easy</u>.

12 I don't <u>rarely</u> <u>worry</u> about my future.

13 They <u>go</u> to bed <u>earlily</u>.

14 The <u>businessman</u> works in the <u>new</u> designed office.

15 His voice <u>is</u> <u>deeply</u>.

type 타이프 치다
really 정말로
secret 비밀
practice 연습하다
burn 타다
designed office 디자인된 사무실

01 다음 중 형용사와 부사가 잘못 짝지어진 것은?

① slow - slowly
② nice - nicely
③ good - goodly
④ bad - badly
⑤ heavy - heavily

02 다음 중 형용사에 ly를 붙여 부사로 만든 것이 아닌 것은?

① perfectly
② safely
③ dangerously
④ early
⑤ kindly

03 다음 중 밑줄 친 부분의 쓰임이 다른 것은?

① He runs <u>fast</u>.
② She studies <u>hard</u>.
③ I can jump <u>high</u>.
④ He speaks English <u>well</u>.
⑤ You are <u>late</u> for school.

04 다음 우리말에 맞도록 ( ) 안에 주어진 단어들을 바르게 나열한 것은?

> 나는 보통 저녁 식사 후에 영어 공부를 한다.
>
> (study, usually, I, dinner, English, after)

① I study usually English after dinner.
② I usually study English after dinner.
③ I study English after usually dinner.
④ Usually study English I after dinner.
⑤ Study English after dinner I usually.

05 다음 중 빈도부사 always의 위치로 알맞은 곳은?

> ① He ② is ③ busy ④ on ⑤ Sunday.

[06–07] 다음 Lisa의 아침 기상 시간표를 보고, 물음에 답하시오.

	Mon.	Tue.	Wed.	Thu.	Fri.	Sat.	Sun.
Time	7:00	7:00	7:00	7:00	7:00	7:00	10:00

항상	always	100%
보통	usually	80%
자주, 종종	often	60~70%
가끔, 때때로	sometimes	50%
거의 ~않다	rarely (seldom)	20%
결코 ~않다	never	0%

06 다음 빈칸에 들어갈 빈도부사로 알맞은 것은?

> Lisa _____ gets up at 7 o'clock in the morning.

① always　　　　② usually
③ often　　　　④ sometimes
⑤ rarely

07 위 시간표에 대한 설명으로 옳지 않은 것은?

① Lisa never gets up at seven thirty.
② Lisa gets up at seven on Friday.
③ Lisa always gets up at seven.
④ Lisa gets up late on Sunday.
⑤ Lisa usually gets up at the same time.

08 다음 빈칸에 들어갈 말로 알맞지 <u>않은</u> 것은?

> She is _____.

① nicely   ② happy
③ bad   ④ kind
⑤ glad

09 다음 중 형용사와 부사의 형태가 같지 <u>않은</u> 것을 고르면?

① fast   ② hard
③ high   ④ late
⑤ quick

10 다음 |보기| 와 같이 빈칸에 알맞은 부사 형태를 쓰시오.

> | 보기 |　easy : easily

(1) beautiful : _____

(2) good : _____

Quiz!

다음 ( ) 안의 말을 알맞은 형태로 바꿔 빈칸을 채워 보자.

1 The train is very _____ . (slow)

2 He solves the problem _____ . (easy)

3 Listen _____ . (careful)

4 She can speak _____ . (fast)

5 This subway is _____ . (dangerous)

6 Tom hits the ball _____ . (nice)

다음 ( ) 안의 우리말 뜻에 해당하는 빈도부사를 빈칸에 채워 보자.

1 I _____ have dinner at 7. (항상)

2 We _____ lie to him. (결코 ~ 않다)

3 Jane can _____ play tennis. (가끔)

다음 ( ) 안의 빈도부사가 들어갈 위치를 골라 보자.

1 My brother ① brushes ② his ③ hair ④. (often)

2 She ① does ② the ③ exercise ④ at ⑤ dawn. (usually)

3 He ① is ② sick ③. (rarely)

4 Mary and Jane ① go ② to ③ the ④ library ⑤. (hardly)

Unit 08

비교

형용사나 부사를 이용하여
다른 것과의 정도 차이를 나타내는 것을
비교라고 하며, 비교 표현에는 원급,
비교급, 최상급 세 가지가 있다.

Unit 08 비교

비교란?

형용사나 부사를 이용하여 다른 것과의 정도 차이를 나타내는 것을 비교라고 하며, 비교 표현에는 원급, 비교급, 최상급 세 가지가 있다.

 1 원급을 이용한 동등비교

비교하는 두 개의 정도가 서로 같을 때
~만큼 ...한 / 하게

| as + 형용사 / 부사 + as |

ex. He is **as tall as** I(me). 그는 나만큼 키가 크다.

 2 비교급을 이용한 우등 비교

두 가지를 비교할 때
더 ~한, 더 ~하게

| 형용사 / 부사 er + than |

ex. He is **taller than** I(me). 그는 나보다 키가 더 크다.

This book is **more** interesting **than** that book. 이 책은 저 책보다 더 재미있다.

 3 최상급을 이용한 비교

세 개 이상 비교할 때
~중에서 가장 …한, 가장 …하게

| (the) 형용사 / 부사 est + in/of |

ex. He is **the tallest** in the class. 그는 반에서 가장 키가 크다.

He is the **most** friendly in the bank.

in + 장소, 범위	~안에서
of + 복수 명사	~중에서

ex. He is the tallest **in** the class.
He is the tallest **of** my brothers.

> **Tip!** 비교대상은 주격이나 목적격을 사용한다. 단 주격으로 사용할 경우 뒤에 동사를 쓸 수 있다.
> *ex.* He is as tall as I am.
> He runs as fast as I do.
> ~~He runs as fast as me do.~~

그는 반에서 가장 키가 크다.

그는 나의 형제들 중에서 가장 키가 크다.

비교급, 최상급 만드는 방법

규칙 변화

종류	공식(비교급/최상급)	원급	비교급	최상급
보통 형용사, 부사	+er/est	small high	smaller higher	smallest highest
e로 끝날 때	+r/st	nice wise	nicer wiser	nicest wisest
'자음 + y'로 끝날 때	y → ier/iest	easy happy	easier happier	easiest happiest
'단모음 + 단자음'으로 끝날 때	마지막 자음을 한 번 더 써주고 + er/est	big hot	bigger hotter	biggest hottest
2음절 중 일부나 3음절 이상의 긴 단어	원급 앞에 more/ most를 써 준다	useful useless foolish famous expensive interesting	**more** useful **more** useless **more** foolish **more** famous **more** expensive **more** interesting	**most** useful **most** useless **most** foolish **most** famous **most** expensive **most** interesting

* '2음절 중 일부'라 함은 -ful, -less, -ish, -ous, -ly로 끝나는 단어를 말한다.

불규칙 변화

원급	비교급	최상급
good, well 좋은, 잘	better	best
bad, ill 나쁜, 병든	worse	worst
many, much 많은	more	most

> **Tip!** 음절(syllables)
> 자음과 모음이 결합해서 소리를 내는 최소한의 단위를 음절이라고 한다. 예를 들면, base는 [b](자음) + [ei](장모음a) + [s](자음)와 같이 자음과 모음이 결합해서 [beis]로 소리나며, 이를 1음절이라고 한다. 또한, 이 base에 ball이 합쳐지면 baseball[béisbɔ:l]로 소리나고 2음절어가 된다. 이렇게 영어에는 1음절에서부터 2음절, 3음절, 4음절 등 다양한 음절의 단어들이 있다.
>
> *ex.* 1음절어 : big, high, nice
> 2음절어 : clev·er, hap·py
> 3음절어 : beau·ti·ful, col·or·ful

다음 형용사나 부사의 비교급과 최상급을 써 보자.

foolish 어리석은
wise 현명한
famous 유명한

1 tall   –   *taller*   –   *tallest*

2 good   –   –

3 happy   –   –

4 strong   –   –

5 fast   –   –

6 foolish –   –

7 well   –   –

8 wise   –   –

9 hot   –   –

10 easy   –   –

11 famous –   –

12 many   –   –

13 useful –   –

14 young   –   –

15 ill   –   –

2

다음 형용사나 부사의 비교급과 최상급을 써 보자.

1	warm	–	*warmer*	–	*warmest*
2	clever	–		–	
3	busy	–		–	
4	beautiful	–		–	
5	small	–		–	
6	nice	–		–	
7	expensive	–		–	
8	interesting	–		–	
9	big	–		–	
10	bad	–		–	
11	light	–		–	
12	pretty	–		–	
13	important	–		–	
14	much	–		–	
15	quick	–		–	

clever 영리한
beautiful 아름다운
interesting 재미있는
important 중요한
quick 빠른

다음 문장에 알맞은 원급, 비교급, 최상급을 골라 동그라미 해 보자.

world 세계
Canada 캐나다
desert 사막
place 장소
score 점수
before 전에

1 My younger sister runs (fast, (faster), fastest) than I.

2 Russia is (big, bigger, the biggest) country in the world.

3 Canada is (large, larger, the largest) than America.

4 She is (beautiful, more beautiful, the most beautiful) than a doll.

5 I am (busy, busier, the busiest) in my family.

6 He is as (strong, stronger, the strongest) as you.

7 This game is as (interesting, more interesting, the most interesting) as that game.

8 She speaks English (good, better, best) than I.

9 Math is as (easy, easier, the easiest) as science.

10 She sings (bad, worse, the worst) than I do.

11 She is the smartest girl (in, of) our school.

12 Desert is (hot, hotter, the hottest) place on the earth.

13 He gets the highest score (in, of) our class.

14 My cat is the fattest (in, of) the three.

15 The weather is getting (bad, worse, the worst) than before.

4

다음 문장에 알맞은 원급, 비교급, 최상급을 골라 동그라미 해 보자.

1 Today is (hot, hotter, the hottest) than yesterday.

2 Your information is (useful, more useful, the most useful) than any other information.

3 She walks as (slow, slower, slowest) as her baby.

4 The chair is as (new, newer, the newest) as the desk.

5 Sujin is the best friend (in, of) my class.

6 The cheetah is (fast, faster, the fastest) among all animals.

7 Your voice is (loud, louder, the loudest) than mine.

8 You are the heaviest (in, of) this town.

9 That bag is (expensive, more expensive, the most expensive) than this.

10 He is the worst (in, of) the three singers.

11 She is as (quick, quicker, the quickest) as a cat.

12 I am the youngest (in, of) my brothers.

13 This book is (boring, more boring, the most boring) than the movie.

14 Writing is (hard, harder, the hardest) than reading.

15 A motorcycle is (dangerous, more dangerous, the most dangerous) than a car.

any other 어떤 다른
information 정보
cheetah 치타
voice 목소리
boring 지루한
writing 쓰기
reading 읽기
motorcycle 오토바이

6 among all animals
모든 동물들 중에서

Unit 08 171

다음 우리말에 알맞게 빈칸을 채워 보자.

earth 지구
difficult 어려운
problem 문제
electric light 전구
bright 밝은
heavy 무거운
brave 용감한
intelligent 머리가 좋은

1 그녀의 엄마는 나의 엄마만큼 젊다.

Her mother is *as young as* my mother.

2 태양이 지구보다 더 크다.

The sun is the earth.

3 이 문제는 저것만큼 어렵다.

This problem is that one.

4 이 전구는 저것보다 더 밝다.

This electric light is that one.

5 철은 나무보다 더 무겁다.

Iron is wood.

6 이 파일은 여섯 개의 파일 중에서 가장 중요하다.

This file is of the six.

7 지하철은 버스보다 더 빠르다.

Subway is bus.

8 그는 4명 중에서 가장 용감하다.

He is the four.

9 복숭아가 사과보다 더 달다.

Peaches are apples.

10 Paul은 우리 학교에서 가장 머리가 좋다.

Paul is our school.

2

다음 우리말에 알맞게 빈칸을 채워 보자.

1 이 장갑은 저 장갑보다 더 따뜻하다.

This glove is *warmer than* that glove.

2 이 약은 저 약만큼 쓰다.

This medicine is that medicine.

3 이 비단은 저 비단보다 더 부드럽다.

This silk is that silk.

4 이것은 저것보다 냄새가 더 고약하다.

This smells that.

5 내 선생님은 학교에서 최고의 선생님이시다.

My teacher is at school.

6 나의 셔츠는 모두 중에서 가장 다채롭다.

My shirt is all.

7 그녀는 세상에서 가장 사랑스러운 인형을 가지고 있다.

She has in the world.

8 이 가방은 저것보다 더 가볍다.

This bag is that.

9 나는 Susan 만큼 현명하게 되기를 바란다.

I want to be Susan.

10 아이들은 어른들보다 영어를 더 빨리 배운다.

Children learn English adults.

---

medicine 약
bitter 쓴
smell 냄새가 나다
bad 나쁜 (고약한)
colorful 다채로운
lovely 사랑스런
wise 현명한, 지혜로운
adult 어른

다음 우리말에 알맞게 빈칸을 채워 보자.

subject 과목
final exam 기말고사
aunt 숙모
island 섬

2 free-freer-freest

1 이 과목은 나에게 가장 쉬운 과목이다.

This subject is _____ *the easiest* _____ subject for me.

2 내 친구는 예전보다 더 한가하다.

My friend is _____ before.

3 그녀는 미래에 더 유명해지고 싶어한다.

She wants to be _____ in the future.

4 그 시험은 기말고사보다 더 어렵다.

The test is _____ the final exam.

5 서울은 홍콩만큼 멋지다.

Seoul is _____ Hong Kong.

6 그 여자 분은 나의 숙모보다 나이가 더 많으시다.

The woman is _____ my aunt.

7 그녀의 손은 얼음만큼 차갑다.

Her hands are _____ ice.

8 그는 나만큼 공부를 잘 한다.

He studies _____ I do.

9 노는 것이 공부하는 것보다 더 쉽다.

Playing is _____ studying.

10 제주도는 한국에서 가장 아름다운 섬이다.

Jeju island is _____ island in Korea.

4

다음 우리말에 알맞게 빈칸을 채워 보자.

1 두 머리가 하나보다 더 낫다. (백짓장도 맞들면 낫다)

Two brains are *better than* one.

2 이 만화 영화는 저 영화만큼 흥미롭다.

This animation is that movie.

3 이번 달은 나에게 최고의 달이다.

This month is for me.

4 너의 필기는 나의 것보다 더 유용하다.

Your note is mine.

5 나는 오늘 최악의 머리스타일을 하고 있다.

I have hair today.

6 고기보다 야채가 너의 몸에 더 좋다.

Vegetables are meat for your health.

7 나는 머리 아픈 것보다 배 아픈 것이 더 심하다.

My stomachache is my headache.

8 이 방은 저 방만큼 어둡다.

This room is that room.

9 백합은 장미만큼 예쁘다.

Lilies are roses.

10 그는 이 마을에서 가장 부자이다.

He is this town.

---

brain 머리, 두뇌
animation 만화 영화
useful 유용한
vegetable 야채
meat 고기
stomachache 위통
headache 두통
lily 백합

다음 밑줄 친 부분들 중에서 **틀린** 곳을 바르게 고쳐 써 보자.

expensive 비싼
friendly 정다운, 상냥한
cold 감기

1 Paul is <u>heaviest</u> than James.
heavier

2 The old woman is <u>the clever</u> <u>of</u> the five.

3 This problem is easier <u>of</u> <u>that</u>.

4 Her father is <u>as</u> <u>taller</u> as my father.

5 It is <u>dark</u> here <u>than</u> there.

6 Picasso is the <u>famousest</u> painter <u>in</u> the world.

7 The building is <u>as</u> <u>higher</u> <u>than</u> the 63 building.

8 The computer is <u>usefuler</u> <u>than</u> this book.

9 He is <u>friendlier</u> <u>than</u> a woman.

10 Mt. Baikdu is <u>the highest</u> mountain <u>of</u> korea.

11 Fire is <u>as</u> <u>more dangerous</u> as water.

12 Hyunwoo is the <u>smartest</u> <u>of</u> his school.

13 I am <u>younger</u> <u>of</u> my brothers.

14 Jane is <u>prettier</u> than <u>your</u>.

15 My cold is getting <u>bader</u> <u>than</u> yesterday.

2

다음 밑줄 친 부분들 중에서 틀린 곳을 바르게 고쳐 써 보자.

1 Jane is <u>more tired</u> <u>he than</u>.
than he

2 He speaks English <u>good</u> than <u>I</u> do.

3 They sell the <u>best</u> cookies <u>in</u> the five bakeries.

4 The cheetah is <u>the</u> <u>faster</u> animal in the world.

5 I have the most <u>wonderful</u> cellphone <u>in</u> the three.

6 Playing sports is <u>most</u> exciting <u>than</u> playing games.

7 L.A. is <u>more warm</u> <u>than</u> New York in December.

8 My new house is <u>big</u> <u>than</u> my old house.

9 I want to be the <u>greater</u> man <u>in</u> the world.

10 January is the <u>coldest</u> month <u>in</u> the year.

11 Lilies smell <u>as</u> <u>best</u> as roses.

12 This watch is <u>expensiver</u> <u>than</u> that.

13 Monday is the <u>busier</u> day <u>of</u> the week.

14 His score is <u>low</u> <u>than</u> yours.

15 What is <u>the</u> <u>happier</u> thing to do?

tired 피곤한
cellphone 휴대전화
smell 냄새나다
score 점수

01 다음 중 원급, 비교급, 최상급의 연결이 바르지 <u>않은</u> 것은?

① small - smaller - smallest
② nice - nicer - nicest
③ high - higher - highest
④ good - gooder - goodest
⑤ happy - happier - happiest

02 다음 각 빈칸에 알맞은 말을 쓰시오.

- The cat is _____ fat _____ the dog.
- I am happier _____ you.
- Peaches are sweeter _____ apples.

03 다음 빈칸에 들어갈 말로 알맞은 것은?

This book is _____ interesting than that one.

① much   ② many
③ more   ④ most
⑤ very

04 우리말과 같은 뜻이 되도록 주어진 단어를 바르게 배열하여 문장을 쓰시오.

수학은 영어만큼 쉽다.

(easy, as, English, as, math, is)

→ _____

[05–06] 다음은 네 친구의 몸무게가 적힌 표이다. 표를 보고 빈칸에 들어갈
친구의 이름을 쓰시오.

Jinjoo	Mina	Kangmin	Woojin
48kg	45kg	45kg	51kg

05 _____ is the heaviest of the four.

06 _____ is as heavy as Kangmin.

07 다음 빈칸에 들어갈 말로 알맞은 것은?

> He is _____ than Jinho.

① light
② lighter
③ more light
④ the lightest
⑤ most light

08 다음 문장에서 <u>틀린</u> 부분을 바르게 고쳐 문장을 다시 쓰시오.

> Seoul is largest city in Korea.
>
> → _____

09 다음 빈칸에 들어갈 말로 바르게 짝지어진 것은?

> · He is the strongest _____ the three.
> · She plays the violin best _____ our school.

① in - in
② in - of
③ of - of
④ of - in
⑤ of - at

10 다음 글을 읽고, 이어지는 문장의 빈칸에 알맞은 말을 고르시오.

> Sujin runs faster than Dongsu.
>
> Dongsu runs faster than Minho.

→ Sujin runs _____ of the three.

① fast   ② faster
③ the fastest   ④ more fast
⑤ the most fast

Quiz!

1 63 building is   building in Seoul. (high)

2 Art is as   as music. (difficult)

3 I am   than you. (busy)

4 Today is   day in this summer. (hot)

5 She speaks English   than he does. (well)

6 America is   than Japan. (large)

7 The apples are as   as pears. (big)

8 My aunt is   than Mrs. Williams. (rich)

9 Sujin is   student in our school. (clever)

10 Paul works as   as Tom. (hard)

11 Rabbits are   than turtles. (fast)

12 This painting is   of all. (colorful)

13 My brother is   than my sister. (tall)

14 She is as   as Judy. (young)

15 He is   guy in the club. (nice)

Grammar **Joy** **2**

- **Review Test 2**
- **내신대비 2**

01 다음 보기에서 알맞은 형용사와 명사를 골라 우리말에 맞게 완성해 보자.

warm, sad, rainy, easy, sick	water, work, movie, day, child

1 따뜻한 물

2 아픈 아이　　　　a

3 슬픈 영화　　　　a

4 쉬운 일　　　　an

5 비오는 날　　　　a

02 다음 주어진 단어를 이용하여 우리말에 맞도록 빈칸에 알맞은 말을 써 보자.

1 This is _____ .

　이것은 매우 어려운 문제이다.　　(very, problem, a, difficult)

2 She is _____ .

　그녀는 나의 여동생이다.　　(my, sister, younger)

3 Bill is _____ .

　Bill은 키가 크고 착한 소년이다.　　(a, boy, tall, good)

4 Jane has _____ .

　Jane은 작고 예쁜 인형들을 가지고 있다.　　(pretty, dolls, small)

5 He lives in _____ .

　그는 크고 오래된 집에서 산다.　　(house, a, old, big)

03 다음 보기에서 알맞은 동사와 형용사를 골라 우리말에 맞게 문장을 완성해 보자.

am, is, are	cold, healthy, hungry, wise, difficult

1 Tom은 현명하다.　　　　Tom 　　　　　　　　　　.

2 그 퀴즈는 어렵다.　　　The quiz 　　　　　　　　　.

3 우리는 건강하다.　　　　We 　　　　　　　　　　　.

4 나는 배고프다.　　　　　I 　　　　　　　　　　　　.

5 춥다.　　　　　　　　　It 　　　　　　　　　　　　.

04 다음 보기에서 알맞은 동사와 형용사를 골라 우리말에 맞게 완성해 보자.

look(s), sound(s), smell(s), taste(s), feel(s)	good, salty, sweet, old, thirsty

1 그 개는 늙어 보인다.　　　The dog 　　　　　　　　　.

2 그 스프는 짠 맛이 난다.　　The soup 　　　　　　　　.

3 그 과자들은 달콤한 냄새가 난다.　The cookies 　　　　　.

4 그 이야기는 좋게 들린다.　　The story 　　　　　　　.

5 나는 목마름을 느낀다. thirsty 목마른　　I 　　　　　　　.

01   다음 (   ) 안에서 알맞은 것을 골라 동그라미 해 보자. (2가지 가능)

1   He buys (some, any) (apple, apples).

2   Can you lend me (some, any) (money, moneys)?

3   I don't want (some, any) (dog, dogs).

4   Do you need (some, any) (coin, coins)?

5   They don't like (some, any) (meat, meats).

6   Jane has (some, any) foreign (friend, friends).

7   Are there (some, any) (leftover, leftovers) in the refrigerator?

foreign friends 외국인 친구   leftover 남은 음식

02   다음 (   ) 안에서 알맞은 것을 골라 동그라미 해 보자.

1   She wears (many, much, a lot of) hairpins.

2   He has (many, much, a lot of) knowledge.   knowledge 지식

3   I don't put (many, much, a lot of) salt in the soup.

4   Uncle drinks (many, much, a lot of) coffee.

5   There are (many, much, a lot of) mosquitos in summer.

6   Tom doesn't need (many, much, a lot of) socks.   sock 양말

7   There is (many, much, a lot of) water in the lake.   lake 호수

03 다음 보기에서 알맞은 것을 고르고 주어진 단어의 알맞은 형태를 빈칸에 써 넣어보자.

> some, any

1 I need _____ . (butter)

2 She doesn't wear _____ . (skirt)

3 Do you have _____ ? (pen)

4 They want _____ . (rice)

5 There isn't _____ in the pot. (water)

6 The woman buys _____ . (orange)

7 Would you like _____ ? (tea)

04 다음 보기에서 알맞은 것을 고르고, 주어진 단어의 알맞은 형태를 빈칸에 써 넣어보자.
(2가지 가능)

> many, much, a lot of

1 She reads _____ . (book)

2 He puts _____ in his coffee. (sugar)

3 _____ dislike vegetable. (child)

4 _____ is needed for success. (effort)

5 There are _____ in the sky. (star)

6 I see _____ in the parking lot. (car)

7 Jenny needs _____ . (help)

dislike 싫어하다   vegetable 야채 effort 노력   needed 필요한   success 성공 help 도움

O1 다음 빈칸에 알맞은 부사를 써 보자.

1	dangerous	위험한	–	위험하게
2	slow	느린	–	느리게
3	beautiful	아름다운	–	아름답게
4	high	높은	–	높게
5	late	늦은	–	늦게
6	heavy	무거운	–	무겁게
7	happy	행복한	–	행복하게
8	early	이른	–	이르게

O2 다음 ( ) 안에 주어진 빈도부사의 위치로 알맞은 곳을 골라 보자.

1 He ① is ② busy ③. (always)

2 They ① like ② pizza ③. (often)

3 Dad ① can ② drive a truck ③. (never)

4 She ① is ② sick ③. (sometimes)

5 I ① know ② the girl ③. (seldom)

03 주어진 단어를 우리말에 알맞게 바꿔 보자.

1 He came _____ . (late)
그는 늦게 왔다.

2 She walks _____ . (fast)
그녀는 빨리 걷는다.

3 Mom drives _____ . (safe)
엄마는 안전하게 운전한다.

4 I go to school _____ . (early)
나는 일찍 학교에 간다.

5 My aunt cooks food _____ . (easy)
내 고모는 음식을 쉽게 요리한다.

04 주어진 빈도부사를 사용하여 우리말에 알맞게 문장을 완성해 보자.

1 Dad _____ busy. (always)
아빠는 항상 바쁘다.

2 I _____ TV. (sometimes)
나는 가끔 TV를 본다.

3 Mom _____ shopping on Friday. (usually)
엄마는 보통 금요일에 쇼핑하러 간다.

4 He _____ the exercise. (hardly)
그는 거의 운동을 하지 않는다.

5 They _____ beef. (never)
그들은 결코 소고기를 먹지 않는다.

01 다음 형용사나 부사의 비교급과 최상급을 써 보자.

	원급	비교급	최상급
1	high		
2	wise		
3	easy		
4	big		
5	foolish		
6	useful		
7	good/well		
8	bad/ill		

02 다음 ( ) 안에서 알맞은 말을 골라 동그라미 해 보자.

1 She is (tall, taller, tallest) than Jimmy.

2 This building is as (high, higher, highest) as the mountain.

3 Bill is (wise, wiser, the wisest) in his class.

4 The cat is as (big, bigger, biggest) as a tiger.

5 The singer is (famous, more famous, the most famous) in the world.

6 Susan plays the violin (well, better, the best) than me.

03 주어진 단어를 변형하여, 우리말에 알맞게 바꿔 보자.

1 The eraser is   yours. (small)

이 지우개는 네 것 만큼 작다.

2 This is   that one. (expensive)

이것은 저것 보다 더 비싸다.

3 Jack is   in his school. (strong)

Jack 은 그의 학교에서 가장 힘이 세다.

4 She swims   me. (fast)

그녀는 나 보다 더 빠르게 수영한다.

5 He plays the piano   Jane. (well)

그는 Jane 만큼 피아노를 잘 친다.

6 The movie is   of the three.
(interesting)

그 영화가 3 개 중에서 가장 재미있다.

7 The baby is   a doll. (pretty)

그 아기는 인형보다 더 예쁘다.

8 Summer is   of 4 seasons in Korea. (hot)

여름이 한국에서는 4 계절 중에서 가장 덥다.

9 He is   celebrities. (famous) celebrities 연예인

그는 연예인들만큼 유명하다.

10 My grade is   Tom's. (bad)

내 성적은 Tom의 성적보다 더 나쁘다.

01 다음 중 형용사가 <u>아닌</u> 것은?

① handsome
② yellow
③ two
④ cloud
⑤ sweet

02 다음 중 순서가 <u>틀리게</u> 배열된 것은?

① the very famous actor
② two tall buildings
③ good my brother
④ the very interesting book
⑤ five small stars

03 다음 명사의 형용사형을 써 보자.

| wind | → _____ 바람이 부는 |
| fog | → _____ 안개가 낀 |

04 다음 밑줄 친 형용사의 쓰임이 보기와 같은 것은?

> The candy is <u>sweet</u>.

① The <u>tall</u> boy is my cousin.
② You look <u>tired</u> today.
③ It is a <u>nice</u> bag.
④ He is my <u>new</u> friend.
⑤ They are <u>happy</u>.

05 다음 우리말에 맞게 짝 지어진 것은?

> 그 이야기는 사실처럼 들린다.
> → The story _____ _____.

① sounds-true
② sounds-truely
③ hears-true
④ hears- fact
⑤ sounds- fact

true 사실인   fact 사실

06 서로 반대되는 뜻을 가진 형용사를 써 보자.

  a. busy   -

  b. tall   -

  c. high   -

  d. hungry -

07 다음 빈칸에 들어갈 말로 알맞지 <u>않은</u> 것은?

> He wants some _____ .

① pens
② coins
③ moneys
④ apples
⑤ water

08 다음 중 빈칸에 들어갈 말이 순서대로 바르게 짝지어진 것은?

> · He doesn't like _____ bread.
>
> · Do you have _____ erasers?
>
> · There is _____ food on the table.

① some - any - any
② any - some - some
③ some - any - some
④ some - some - any
⑤ any - any - some

09 다음 중 <u>틀린</u> 부분을 바르게 고쳐 문장을 다시 써 보자.

> The man drinks many milk every day.

⇨ _____

_____

10 다음 우리말을 영어로 바르게 옮긴 것은?

> 창고에는 많은 쌀이 있다.

① There is a lot of rice in the storage.
② There is much rices in the storage.
③ There is many rices in the storage.
④ There are a lot of rice in the storage.
⑤ There are much rices in the storage.

storage 창고

11 다음 빈칸에 공통으로 들어갈 수 있는 말을 고르면?

> He has _____ caps.
> 그는 많은 모자를 가지고 있다.
> Elephants drink _____ water.
> 코끼리들은 많은 물을 마신다.

① many
② much
③ a lot of
④ some
⑤ any

12 다음 밑줄 친 부사의 쓰임이 예문과 같은 것은?

> Tom is a <u>very</u> kind boy.

① She walks <u>very</u> slowly.
② He has two <u>very</u> big dogs.
③ Mom cooks <u>very</u> easily.
④ Uncle eats <u>very</u> fast.
⑤ Jane likes music <u>very</u> much.

13 다음 형용사-부사가 <u>틀리게</u> 짝지어진 것은?

① safe - safely
② quick - quickly
③ easy - easily
④ fast - fast
⑤ late - lately

14 주어진 단어를 알맞게 나열해 보자.

> man a fat very

_____

15 주어진 단어를 더해서 올바른 문장을 만들어
보자.

> I get an egg. (very, fresh)

① I get an fresh very egg.
② I get an very fresh egg.
③ I get a fresh very egg.
④ I get a very fresh egg.
⑤ I get an egg very fresh.

fresh 신선한

16 다음 중 틀린 곳을 찾아 바르게 고쳐 보자.

> It looks very nicely.

_____ ⇨ _____

17 다음 중 어법상 옳지 않은 것은?

① She is always happy.
② He goes sometimes to the library.
③ I will never talk with him.
④ They often play a ball.
⑤ Tom rarely goes out.

18 다음 형용사–부사가 잘못 짝지어진 것은?

① high - high
② good - goodly
③ late - late
④ early - early
⑤ fast - fast

19 빈칸에 들어갈 수 있는 것 두 개를 고르면?

> She doesn't _____ go
> camping.

① rarely
② seldom
③ never
④ usually
⑤ sometimes

[20~21] 다음 표를 보고 아래질문에 답해 보자.

	키	몸무게	나이
Ann	153 cm	43 kg	12살
Bill	149 cm	41 kg	10살
Susan	147 cm	52 kg	11살

20 다음 중 옳은 것은?

① Ann is as tall as Susan.
② Bill is heavier than Ann.
③ Bill is older than Ann.
④ Susan is older than Bill.
⑤ Ann is as fat as Susan.

21 앞의 표의 내용과 일치하도록 두 개 고르면?

> Susan is (taller, heavier, younger) than Ann.

22 주어진 단어를 이용하여 빈칸을 채워 보자.

> Mary and Jenny are the same age.
> Jenny is _____ _____
> _____ Mary. (old)

23 다음 빈칸에 들어갈 말이 맞게 짝지어진 것은?

> Tom is the strongest _____ his class.
> Jane is the wisest _____ the five girls.

① in - in
② of - of
③ in - of
④ of - in
⑤ at - in

24 다음 두 문장이 같은 뜻이 되도록 할 때, 빈칸에 알맞은 말은?

> Tom is taller than Jane.
> = Jane is _____ than Tom.

① fatter
② younger
③ better
④ shorter
⑤ longer

25 다음 빈칸에 알맞지 <u>않은</u> 것은?

> This is more _____ than that.

① interesting
② delicious
③ famous
④ happy
⑤ popular

popular 인기있는

Grammar **Joy** 2

1·2회

종합문제

01 다음 두 문장이 같은 뜻이 되도록 빈칸에 알맞은 말을 쓰시오.

> There are five rabbits in this farm.
> = _____ in this farm.

02 다음 문장을 부정문으로 바꿔 쓰시오.

> There is a clock on the TV.
> = _____
>
> _____

03 다음 문장 중 바르지 <u>않은</u> 것은?

① There is a hat on the table.
② There is five trees at the park.
③ There is not an eraser in the pencil case.
④ There are some sheep on the hill.
⑤ There are two banks on the street.

[04–05] 다음을 읽고, 물음에 답하시오.

> _____ A bear is in the river. Three monkeys are by the tree, and two deer are by the tree, too. There are some rabbits, zebras, and birds in the field.

04 위 글의 빈칸에 들어갈 말로 어법상 알맞은 것은? (2개)

① In this picture many animals are.
② A lot of animals there are in this picture.
③ In this picture is many animals.
④ There are a lot of animals in this picture.
⑤ A lot of animals are in this picture.

05 다음 질문에 알맞은 답을 모두 고르면?

> Is there a bear on the tree?

① Yes, there are
② No, it isn't.
③ Yes, there is.
④ No, there isn't.
⑤ No, there aren't.

06 다음 빈칸에 들어갈 말로 바르지 <u>않은</u> 것은?

> _____ watch the
> soccer game on TV.

① He and I
② Tom
③ We
④ Mr. and Mrs. Kim
⑤ Her brothers

08

> · He _____ a car.
> · We _____ our teacher.

① drive - help
② drive - helps
③ drives - help
④ drives - helps
⑤ drove - helps

09 다음 중 3인칭 단수 일반동사의 현재형을 만드는 방법이 <u>다른</u> 것은?

① wash
② like
③ eat
④ take
⑤ love

[07–08] 다음 빈칸에 들어갈 말이 순서대로 바르게 짝지어진 것을 고르시오.

> Mr. Brown _____ a bath
> every day. Sometimes, he
> and his son _____ a bath
> together.

07
① take - take
② take - takes
③ takes - take
④ takes - takes
⑤ takes - taking

10 다음 밑줄 친 부분 중 바르지 <u>않은</u> 것은?

① Jane <u>goes</u> to church.
② He <u>looks</u> at the picture.
③ My brothers <u>play</u> soccer.
④ The girl <u>smiles</u> at me.
⑤ They <u>watches</u> the soccer game.

11 다음 빈칸에 들어갈 말이 순서대로 바르게 짝 지어진 것은?

> A : ___ⓐ___ Mr. Smith give you some flowers?
>
> B : No, he ___ⓑ___ . He ___ⓒ___ me some chocolate.

	ⓐ	ⓑ	ⓒ
①	Do	- doesn't	- give
②	Does	- doesn't	- gives
③	Does	- does	- give
④	Do	- does	- gives
⑤	Does	- doesn't	- give

12 다음 문장 중 바른 것은?

① Paul doesn't waits for the school bus.
② She doesn't write a letter.
③ My son doesn't eats lemons.
④ The boy doesn't swims in the sea.
⑤ He and she don't goes to the park.

13 다음 문장에서 <u>틀린</u> 부분을 바르게 고쳐 쓰시오.

> Does Tom and she read the book?

_____ ⇨ _____

14 다음 빈칸에 알맞은 말을 쓰시오.

> • She loves her dad. And he loves her, _____.
> • I don't eat carrots. And my brother doesn't eat carrots, _____.

15 다음 대화의 빈칸에 들어갈 말이 순서대로 바르게 짝지어진 것은?

> A : _____ your brothers play tennis?
>
> B : Yes, _____ .

① Do - they do
② Is - he is
③ Does - he does
④ Are - they are
⑤ Does - they do

16 다음 중 동사원형과 –ing형이 바르지 <u>않은</u> 것은?

① meet - meeting
② wax - waxing
③ eat - eating
④ cook - cooking
⑤ study - studiing

19 다음 중 밑줄 친 부분의 쓰임이 바른 것은?

① He <u>is believing</u> Tom.
② I'<u>m needing</u> a new computer.
③ The dog <u>is hating</u> the cat.
④ Mary <u>is cooking</u> dinner.
⑤ Jinsu <u>is knowing</u> me.

17 다음 질문에 대한 대답으로 알맞은 것은?

> A : Is she listening to the radio?
>
> B : _____

① Yes, she is.
② Yes, she does.
③ No, she doesn't.
④ Yes, she was.
⑤ No, she wasn't.

20 다음은 현재 시제를 현재진행형으로 바꾼 문장이다. <u>틀린</u> 부분을 바르게 고쳐 쓰시오.

> Sumi and Tom drink some milk.
> → Sumi and Tom drinking some
>   milk now.

_____ ⇨ _____

18 다음 문장을 부정문으로 만들 때, not이 들어갈 위치로 알맞은 곳은?

> ① We ② are ③ eating
> ④ cookies ⑤.

01 다음 단어들의 관계가 같도록 빈칸에 알맞은 말을 쓰시오.

old : young	difficult :
sun : sunny	wind :

02 다음 중 빈칸에 들어갈 말로 바르지 <u>않은</u> 것은?

Jack is a _____ boy.

① very
② kind
③ smart
④ tall
⑤ handsome

03 다음 우리말과 같은 뜻이 되도록 ( ) 안의 단어를 순서대로 바르게 배열한 것은?

4권의 두꺼운 영어책이 있다.
→ There are (four, books, thick, English).

① thick English four books
② English thick four books
③ four thick English books
④ thick four English books
⑤ four English thick books

04 다음 문장 중 바른 것은?

① This is very a nice car.
② It is new my MP3 player.
③ These are beautiful two pictures.
④ That is a my coat.
⑤ They are very tall boys.

05 다음 대화의 빈칸에 알맞은 말을 쓰시오.

A : Are you hungry?
B : No, I'm not. I'm _____.
(배가 불러)

06 다음 빈칸에 들어갈 말로 알맞은 것은?

I have some _____.

① candy
② toy
③ ball
④ rulers
⑤ eraser

07 다음 중 밑줄 친 부분의 쓰임이 잘못된 것은?

① Do they have <u>any</u> homework to do?
② He doesn't open <u>some</u> windows.
③ I meet <u>some</u> painters.
④ She doesn't drink <u>any</u> water all day.
⑤ Do you play <u>any</u> computer games?

08 some과 any 중에서 다음 빈칸에 공통으로 들어갈 말을 쓰시오.

- There are _____ cows in the farm.
- Would you like _____ coffee?

09 다음 문장에서 틀린 부분을 찾아 바르게 고쳐 쓰시오.

A lot of banana are in the basket.

_____ ⇨ _____

10 다음 빈칸에 들어갈 말로 알맞은 것은?

She doesn't sell much _____.

① salt
② apples
③ roses
④ rings
⑤ onions

11 다음 빈칸에 들어갈 말이 순서대로 바르게 짝지어진 것은?

Ted : What are you doing?
Lisa : I'm making _____ cakes.
Ted : Oh, I like your cakes. What are you mixing?
Lisa : _____ flour, _____ butter and water.

① many - any - some
② many - a lot of - some
③ much - much - any
④ much - a lot of - any
⑤ a lot of - much - some

12 다음 밑줄 친 말을 대신할 수 있는 말을 쓰시오.

> There are <u>many</u> cookies in the box.

_____

[13~14] 다음을 읽고, 물음에 답하시오.

> Tom has ____ⓐ____ work. He needs ____ⓑ____ time to finish it. <u>He helps much friends.</u> But there is no friend to help him. So he is unhappy now.

13 위 글의 빈칸 ⓐ, ⓑ에 들어갈 말이 순서대로 바르게 짝지어진 것은?

① many - much
② many - a lot of
③ much - many
④ a lot of - many
⑤ a lot of - a lot of

14 위 글의 밑줄 친 문장에서 <u>틀린</u> 부분을 고쳐 쓰시오.

_____ ⇨ _____

15 다음 문장 중 바르지 <u>않은</u> 것을 고르시오.

① There are much rice in the bag.
② I spend a lot of money.
③ Does he want a lot of cheese?
④ He doesn't buy much salt.
⑤ We have a lot of snow.

16 다음 중 정도에 따른 빈도부사가 올바른 순서로 배열된 것은?

① always > never > sometimes > rarely > usually > often
② never > usually > rarely > sometimes > always > often
③ usually > sometimes > always > often > rarely > never
④ often > always > usually > rarely > sometimes > never
⑤ always > usually > often > sometimes > rarely > never

17 다음 중 빈도부사의 위치가 바르지 <u>않은</u> 것은?

① He always remembers you.
② She often smiles.
③ It's often very hot in summer.
④ He washes never his car.
⑤ She usually goes to church by car.

19 다음 Jenny의 시간표를 보고 빈칸에 알맞은 빈도부사를 쓰시오.

class	Mon.	Tue.	Wed.
1	Math	English	History
2	English	Science	English
3	Music	Art	Science
4			Korean

class	Thu.	Fri.
1	Math	Science
2	Korean	English
3	English	Math
4		Korean

Jenny _____ has English
class.

18 다음 | 보기 | 와 같이 형용사의 부사형을 쓰시오.

| 보기 | late - late

(1) early   - _____

(2) hard   - _____

20 다음 빈칸에 들어갈 말로 알맞은 것은?

She crosses the street _____.

① good
② easy
③ carefully
④ dangerous
⑤ safe

MEMO

MEMO

MEMO

Grammar joy Answer

2

01 There is~, There are~

p.14~17

① 1 is 2 are 3 is 4 is ▶우유와 같이 셀 수 없는 명사는 단수 취급한다. 5 are ▶우유는 셀 수 없는 명사지만 단위명사로 양을 나타낼 경우에는 셀 수 있다. 6 are 7 is 8 is 9 are 10 is ▶food는 셀 수 없는 명사이므로 There is가 온다. 11 are 12 is ▶something은 단수. 13 is 14 are ▶a spoon and a fork는 복수이므로 There are가 온다. 15 are

② 1 is 2 are 3 are 4 are 5 is 6 is 7 are ▶bread는 셀 수 없는 명사이지만 단위 명사 leaf를 사용한 four loaves는 네 덩어리를 나타내므로 There are가 온다. 8 are 9 are 10 is 11 are 12 is 13 is 14 are 15 is

③
1 There are three pencils
2 There are five hairdressers
3 There is a film festival
4 There is a lot of salt
5 There are two pillows
6 There is some tea
7 There are a lot of people
8 There is a convenience store
9 There is a mountain
10 There is something

④
1 Are there, there are
2 Is there, there isn't
3 There aren't
4 Is there, there is
5 Are there, there aren't
6 Is there, there is
7 There aren't
8 There isn't

p.18~19

①
1 There are 2 There are
3 There aren't 4 There isn't
5 There isn't 6 There is
7 There isn't 8 There aren't
9 There isn't 10 There are

②
1 Some tennis balls are 2 There is a university
3 Five events are 4 There is a jumper
5 There is a lot of rice
▶rice는 셀 수 없는 명사로, 단수 취급하므로 is가 온다.
6 Five oceans are 7 Some food is
8 There are seven Italian restaurants
9 There is a man 10 A free coupon is

p.20~21

① 1 is → are 2 are → is 3 is → are 4 isn't → aren't 5 is → are 6 are → is ▶셀 수 없는 명사(cheese)는 단수취급. 7 is → are ▶cheese는 셀 수 없는 명사이지만 치즈 조각들은 셀 수 있으므로 is가 아닌 are을 써야한다. 8 man → men 9 hour → hours 10 is → are 11 are → is ▶trash는 셀 수 없는 명사이므로 is를 써야한다. 12 are → is 13 is → are 14 peoples → people 15 boards → board

② 1 is → are 2 crab → crabs ▶동사가 are이므로 주어는 복수인 crabs가 온다. 3 is → are 4 is → are 5 are → is 6 are → is 7 dancer → dancers 8 are → is 9 is → are 10 are → is 11 are → is 12 is → are 13 dog → dogs 14 class → classes ▶calss는 s로 끝났으므로 es를 붙여 복수형을 만든다. s, o, x, sh, ch로 끝나는 명사는 es를 붙여 복수형을 만든다. 15 is → are

01 ② 02 ⑤ 03 ③ 04 ② 05 ③ 06 ④
07 are - is 08 There isn't a baby by the sofa.
09 ② 10 Are there three butterflies in the garden?

01 There is, There are뒤에 오는 명사가 단수인지 복수인지 확인한다. ①③④⑤는 복수, ②는 단수이므로 There is 뒤에 들어갈 수 있는 것은 ②이다.

02 Is there~?로 물으면 Yes, there is. / No, there isn't로. Are there~?로 물으면 Yes, there are / No, there aren't로 대답하여 be동사로 시작하는 질문은 반드시 Yes~, No~로 대답한다.

03 some water는 셀 수 없는 명사이므로 there뒤에 is가 와야 한다.

04 three cats는 복수이므로 복수동사 are로 받는다.

05 ①②④⑤는 '~있다'는 의미의 be 동사 is이고, ③는 '~이다'라는 의미의 be동사이다.

07 There 뒤의 be동사는 주어에 따라 달라진다.

08 There is~의 부정문은 be동사 뒤에 not을 붙이면 된다.

09 주어가 셀 수 있는 복수명사일 때는 "There are~"를, 셀 수 없는 명사일 때는 "There is~"를 사용한다.

10 There is(are)로 시작하는 문장의 의문문은 be동사를 문장 맨 앞으로 보내면 된다.

p.26

1 There is a lot of water
2 There isn't a map
3 There are 12 months
4 There is some bread
5 There isn't a spider
6 There is a lot of snow
7 There are four Sundays
8 There is some coffee
9 There is a lot of flour
  ▶flour는 셀 수 없는 명사이므로 단수 취급하여 There is가 온다.
10 There isn't a dog

02 일반동사의 긍정문

① 1 pushes 2 likes 3 sits 4 catches
5 passes 6 holds 7 washes 8 tries 9 replies
10 works 11 says 12 asks 13 takes
14 sends 15 waxes 16 coaches 17 cries
18 comes 19 misses 20 reads 21 does ▶do는 조동사로 쓰이지만 일반동사로도 쓰여서 '~하다'라는 의미를 지닌다.
22 prays 23 plays 24 teaches 25 touches
26 tells 27 mixes 28 waxes 29 sees
30 pitches

② 1 meets 2 walks 3 flies 4 hits
5 finishes 6 loves 7 passes 8 hears 9 has
10 tosses 11 solves 12 plays 13 fries
14 matches 15 guesses 16 eats 17 watches
18 writes 19 fixes 20 draws 21 begins
22 pushes 23 goes 24 enjoys 25 pays
26 hates 27 studies 28 stays 29 kisses
30 lives

③ 1 have 2 does 3 study 4 go 5 learns
6 has ▶The house는 3인칭 단수이므로 has를 쓴다. 7 brings
8 open ▶The students는 복수이므로 open에 s를 붙이지 않는다.
9 moves 10 catches 11 grows 12 close
13 likes 14 takes 15 visit

④ 1 tosses 2 push 3 teaches 4 finish
5 do 6 gives 7 listen 8 takes 9 lives
10 clean 11 eats 12 lives 13 wants 14 hear
15 looks

⑤ 1 My mom 2 We 3 She 4 They 5 Paul
6 John 7 He 8 We 9 Jane and Judy 10 We
11 My aunt 12 The tiger 13 It 14 You
15 He and she

6 1 Jim 2 My friend 3 Mary and Joe
4 He 5 I 6 The scientists 7 They 8 He 9 You
10 The man 11 She 12 A day 13 The children
14 The couples ▶couple은 둘을 하나로 묶어서 생각하므로 단수
취급하고 couples는 복수 취급한다. 15 Mike

꼭꼭 다지기   p.36~39

1 1 reads 2 loses 3 sends 4 remember ▶
Her brothers는 복수이므로 동사에 s를 붙이지 않는다. 5 fly
6 washes 7 know 8 change ▶grandparents는 복수이
므로 동사에 s를 붙이지 않는다. 9 speaks 10 feels
11 touches 12 arrive 13 buy 14 have
15 waxes

2 1 go 2 makes 3 does 4 leave 5 tries
6 pray 7 matches 8 hurries 9 drive 10 hates
11 give 12 pay 13 dries 14 gets 15 enjoy
▶The young men은 the young man의 복수형이므로 동사에 s를 붙이
지 않는다.

3 1 carries 2 hope 3 sounds 4 says
5 catches 6 kisses 7 have 8 eat 9 has
10 pull 11 sings 12 travels 13 does 14 look
15 fries

4 1 spend 2 thinks 3 finishes 4 pays
5 do 6 bites 7 keeps 8 has 9 study
10 mixes ▶Mom은 3인칭 단수이므로 동사에 es를 붙인다.
11 misses 12 get 13 rains 14 take 15 tries

실력 다지기   p.40~41

1 1 take → takes 2 do → does 3 The boys
→ The boy 4 close → closes 5 cross → crosses
6 drys → dries 7 jumps → jump 8 end → ends
9 trys → tries 10 begin → begins 11 fixs →
fixes 12 pass → passes 13 The kid → The kids
14 hugs → hug 15 repeats → repeat

2 1 boys → boy 2 pay → pays 3 wear →
wears 4 haves → has 5 The girls → The girl
6 tigers → tiger 7 shines → shine 8 cooks →
cook 9 take → takes 10 baby → babies
11 catchs → catches 12 wants → want 13 sells
→ sell 14 replys → replies 15 erase → erases

실전Test   p.42~45

01 ④ 02 ③ 03 ① 04 ① 05 ①
06 go, shows, plays, have, sings 07 ⑤
08 ④ 09 likes 10 ⑤

01 일반동사에 s, es를 붙일 때 [자음+y]로 끝나는 동사는 y를 i로 고치
고 es를 붙인다.

02 일반동사에 s, es를 붙일 때 x로 끝나는 동사는 es를 붙이고 e로 끝
나는 동사는 s만 붙인다.

03 주어가 1인칭, 2인칭(단수, 복수), 3인칭 복수일 때는 일반동사에 s,
es를 붙이지 않는다.

04 일반동사에 s, es를 붙일 때 sh로 끝나는 동사는 es를 붙인다.

05 [모음+y]로 끝나는 동사는 3인칭 단수형으로 만들 때 s만 붙인다.
My brother는 3인칭 단수이므로 buy → buys, Mary and John은
3인칭 복수이므로 동사에 s, es를 붙일 필요가 없다.

06 주어가 1인칭, 2인칭(단수, 복수), 3인칭 복수일 경우에는 일반동사
에 s나 es를 붙이지 않으며, 3인칭 단수일 경우에만 s, es를 붙인다.

07 주어가 3인칭 단수이므로 일반동사에 s나 es를 붙여야 한다.

08 일반동사의 3인칭 단수 현재형을 만들 때 [자음+y]로 끝난 동사는 y
를 i로 고치고 es를 붙이고, [모음+y]로 끝나는 동사는 그대로 s만
붙인다.

09 주어가 3인칭 단수이므로 likes에 s를 붙여 사용한다.

10 동사(help)에 s가 붙어 있으므로 주어는 3인칭 단수가 와야 한다.

Quiz!   p.46

1 You 2 They 3 He 4 Her sister 5 We
6 This man 7 Ann

1 loves 2 play 3 has 4 reads 5 finish
6 take 7 sells 8 goes

03 일반동사의 부정문과 의문문

p.50~55

1 1 don't, tell 2 don't, dive 3 don't, buy
4 doesn't, snow 5 doesn't, drive 6 don't, look
7 doesn't, have 8 don't, order 9 doesn't, feed
10 don't, like ▶My daughters 3인칭 복수이므로, don't를 써서 부정문을 만든다. 11 doesn't, eat 12 doesn't, ride
13 don't, talk ▶주어 Sally and I는 두 명을 나타내므로, 복수형이 되어, don't를 써서 부정문을 만든다. 14 doesn't, do
15 don't, take

2 1 Do, know 2 Does, enter 3 Does, sit
4 Do, take 5 Does, come 6 Do, like ▶주어 the students는 3인칭 복수이므로, Do를 사용하여 의문문을 만든다.
7 Does, teach 8 Does, invite 9 Do, sing ▶Woman 은 단수, Women은 복수이다. 10 Does, pay 11 Does, go
12 Do, draw 13 Do, wear ▶Judy and Mary는 3인칭 복수 이므로 Do를 사용하여 의문문을 만든다. 14 Does, open
15 Does, stand

3 1 doesn't, move 2 Does, push
3 doesn't, learn 4 Does, turn 5 doesn't, shake
6 doesn't ,tear 7 Do, build 8 Does, wear
9 doesn't, belong 10 Do, catch 11 don't, have
12 Does , live 13 don't, collect 14 Does, bring
15 don't, do

4 1 too 2 either 3 either 4 either 5 too
6 either 7 too 8 too 9 either 10 too ▶긍정문에 는 too, 부정문에는 either를 쓴다.

5 1 doesn't, prepare 2 Does, open
3 doesn't, start 4 don't, grow 5 Do, understand
6 don't, go 7 doesn't, capture 8 Does, have ▶주 어 it은 3인칭 단수형이다. 9 don't, hate 10 Does, take

6 1 don't, take 2 Does, chat 3 Does, snow
4 doesn't, remember 5 Do, exercise
6 doesn't, chew 7 don't, turn 8 Do, look
9 Does, solve ▶3인칭 단수형 solves는 solve에 s가 붙은 것이므로, 원형은 s를 뺀 solve로 써야 한다. 10 don't, set

p.56~59

1
1 He doesn't wait
2 Does the frog sing
3 They don't mix
4 Do he and she believe
5 Mrs. Park doesn't have
6 She doesn't iron
7 Does Matt build
8 Do you count
9 His brothers don't work
10 Does mom make

2
1 Do Tom and John trust
2 They don't remember
3 She doesn't eat
4 Does Judy fry
5 she doesn't forget
6 Paul doesn't play
7 Mom doesn't nag
8 Do his parents buy ▶주어 parents가 3인칭이지만 복수형이 므로, Do를 이용하여 의문문을 만든다.
9 We don't take
10 He doesn't walk

3 1 she does 2 she doesn't 3 it does
4 I do 5 she doesn't 6 they do 7 he does
8 they don't 9 I don't 10 she doesn't

4 1 too 2 either 3 too 4 too 5 either
6 either 7 too 8 either 9 too 10 either

1
1 gives → give   2 don't → doesn't   3 sell
not → don't sell   4 flies → fly   5 don't → doesn't
6 do → does   7 Is → Does   8 isn't → doesn't
9 Does → Do   10 have not → don't have
11 meets → meet   12 Are → Do   13 don't →
doesn't   14 Does → Do   15 too → either

2
1 Do → Does   2 isn't → doesn't   3 Do →
Does   4 goes → go   5 Does → Do   6 either →
too   7 Are → Do   8 has not → doesn't have ▶have
나 has의 부정은 don't have나 doesn't have이다.   9 worries →
worry   10 are → do   11 Does → Do   12 doesn't
→ don't   13 aren't → don't   14 walks → walk
15 is → does

3
1 take / 일반동사. I don't take
2 is / be동사. Is she, she isn't
   ▶be동사의 의문문을 만들 때는 be동사를 주어 앞으로 보낸다.
3 climb / 일반동사. They don't climb
4 are / be동사. Sumi and Jane aren't
   ▶be동사의 부정문을 만들 때는 be동사 뒤에 not을 붙인다.
5 is / be동사. Is his age, it isn't.
6 buy / 일반동사. Do his parents buy, they do
7 are / be동사. Are those books, they aren't
8 is / be동사. Dad isn't
9 makes / 일반동사. Does he make, he does
10 are / be동사. Are you, I'm not.

4
1 brushes / 일반동사. Does Suji brush, she does
2 is / be동사. Is that, it isn't
   ▶be동사로 묻는 질문에는 be동사로 답한다.
3 goes / 일반동사. Does Sam go, he does.
   ▶do나 does로 묻는 질문에는 do나 does로 답한다.
4 are / be동사. They aren't

5 cries / 일반동사. The baby doesn't cry
6 peels / 일반동사. Does the girl peel, she does
7 is / be동사. Is this, it isn't
8 is / be동사. She isn't
9 rings / 일반동사. He doesn't ring
10 play / 일반동사. We don't play

실전Test

01 ①   02 ②   03 I don't write an answer on
the board.   04 ①   05 ⑤   06 ⑤   07 ②
08 Do the students play baseball after
school?   09 ⑤   10 ③

01 don't, doesn't 뒤에는 동사원형이 오게 되므로 cooks는 cook이 된
   다.
02 주어인 your father가 3인칭 단수이므로 Does를 사용하고, does
   뒤에는 동사원형을 쓴다. 대답할 때도 주어가 3인칭 단수이므로
   doesn't를 사용한다.
03 일반동사의 부정문은 doesn't나 don't를 동사 앞에 붙여서 만든다. I
   는 1인칭 단수이므로 don't 를 사용한다.
04 Do로 물어 보면 do나 don't로, Does로 물어보면 does나 doesn't로
   대답한다.
05 ①doesn't 뒤에는 동사원형이 온다. teaches → teach ②일반동사의
   부정문은 don't나 doesn't를 사용한다. ③you는 2인칭이므로 Do를
   이용하여 의문문을 만든다. ④Does뒤에는 동사원형이 온다. sells
   → sell
06 Yes, he does가 되어야 한다.
07 ①③④⑤는 일반 동사의 의문문으로 조동사does가 필요하지만 ②는
   be동사 의문문으로 '그는 학교 선생님이니?'라는 질문이므로 be동사
   is가 와야 한다.
08 The students가 3인칭 복수이므로 Do를 주어 앞으로 보내서 의문
   문을 만들어야 한다.
09 ①②③④는 긍정문이므로 too, ⑤는 부정문이므로 either를 사용한
   다.
10 Peter는 그녀를 기다리지 않는다. Eric도 역시 그녀를 기다리지 않
   는다. 그러므로 둘 다 그녀를 기다리지 않는다.

p.68

1 Do you make your dress?

2 Mrs. Kim doesn't go outside.

3 Does he take a walk every day?

4 We don't clean our classroom.

5 Do her children eat a snack between meals?

6 Does it rain?

7 He doesn't kick a ball.

8 She and I don't send and receive text message.

9 Does the tree have a lot of apples?

10 Do they email Jane?

04 현재진행형

p.72~75

1

1 현재형, 공부한다 / 현재진행형형, 공부하고 있다.

2 현재진행형, 그리고 있다 / 현재형, 그린다

3 현재형, 일한다 / 현재진행형, 일하고 있다

4 현재형, 센다 / 현재진행형, 세고 있다

5 현재진행형, 요리하고 있다 / 현재형, 요리한다

2 1 running ▶'단모음(1개 모음)+단자음(1개 자음)'으로 끝나는 동사는 마지막 자음을 하나 더 써 주고 ing를 붙. 2 opening
3 standing 4 dropping 5 trying 6 tying
7 lying 8 playing 9 getting 10 riding
11 writing 12 dying 13 studying 14 waxing
15 stopping ▶'단모음+단자음'으로 끝나는 동사는 마지막 자음을 하나 더 써 주고 ing를 붙인다. 16 watching
17 speaking ▶[2개모음+1개 자음]으로 끝나는 동사는 ing를 붙인다. 18 crying 19 chatting 20 working
21 drawing 22 visiting 23 coming 24 using
25 listening 26 washing 27 beginning ▶'단모음+단자음'으로 끝나는 동사는 마지막 자음을 하나 더 써 주고 ing를 붙인다.
28 waiting 29 eating ▶'2개 모음+1개 자음'으로 끝나는 동사는 ing를 붙인다. 30 singing

3 1 skiing 2 beginning 3 teaching
4 saying 5 tying 6 having 7 drawing
8 driving 9 fixing 10 mixing 11 sitting
12 flying 13 tearing 14 putting 15 swimming
16 opening 17 dying 18 cutting 19 enjoying
20 washing 21 listening 22 dancing
23 telling 24 lying 25 coming 26 stopping
27 waiting 28 visiting 29 winning 30 frying

4 1 am flying 2 are cutting 3 are watering
4 is sitting 5 is waxing 6 is eating
7 are making 8 is looking 9 is going
10 are playing

1 1 현재진행형. is snowing 2 현재진행형. are making
▶Sujin and I는 복수이므로 be동사는 are을 쓴다. 3 현재진행형. is
looking at 4 현재형. play 5 현재진행형. is snoring
6 현재진행형. are taking 7 현재진행형. is flying 8 현재형.
quits 9 현재진행형. is lying 10 현재형. skate

2 1 현재형. walks 2 현재진행형. is blowing 3 현재
형. moves ▶객관적 사실은 현재형으로 나타낸다. 4 현재진행형.
are carrying 5 현재진행형. is watching 6 현재형. use
7 현재진행형. is dying 8 현재형. keeps 9 현재진행형. is
tying 10 현재진행형. is hunting

3
1 Are you enjoying
2 Your daughter isn't cleaning
3 I'm not dreaming
4 Is my aunt sewing
5 Is she sweeping
6 The stars aren't shining
7 Is he cooking
8 Are they reading
9 Are Koreans wearing
10 The kid isn't eating

4 1 she is 2 they aren't 3 they are
4 I'm not 5 it is 6 he is 7 they aren't 8 it isn't
9 he is 10 they aren't

1
1 현재형. Do you hate, I do
2 현재진행형. Is the sun rising, it isn't
3 현재진행형. Mom isn't washing
4 현재형. Does the bus go, it does
5 현재진행형. He isn't listening

6 현재형. People don't run
7 현재진행형. Are your parents shopping?, they aren't
8 현재형. Does Jane stand, she does
9 현재진행형. I'm not writing
10 현재형. Does the man sleep, he doesn't

2
1 현재진행형. Is she waxing, she is
2 현재진행형. We aren't working
3 현재형. Does he snore, he doesn't
4 현재진행형. Your dad isn't playing
5 현재형. The girls don't ski
6 현재진행형. Is the lady trying on, she is
7 현재형. Do you worry about, I do
8 현재진행형. My sisters aren't dancing
9 현재형. The penguin doesn't swim
10 현재형. Do they have, they don't

3 1 riding → am riding 2 is needing → needs
▶need는 현재진행형으로 만들 수 없는 동사 3 eat → eating
▶eat의 ing형은 '2개모음+1개자음'으로 끝났으므로 eating이다.
4 Does → Is 5 do → am 6 is wanting → wants
7 is → are 8 touring → are touring 9 repairs →
is repairing 10 calling → am calling

4 1 Does → Is ▶진행형의 의문문에는 do, does가 필요 없다.
2 take → taking 3 is forgetting → forgets 4 use
→ using 5 having → is having 6 am drinking →
drink 7 Do → Are 8 doesn't → isn't 9 is wear
→ are wearing 10 don't → am not

실전Test

01 ③ 2 ⑤ 3 ⑤ 4 ② 5 He isn't working
at his office. 6 ③ 7 ④ 8 I dance in my
room. 9 She washes her hands. 10 ②

01 현재진행형은 'be동사+동사원형-ing'이며, 둘 다 3인칭 단수이므로
is를 사용한다.

02 ① [2개모음+1개자음]으로 끝나면 그대로 ing만 붙여 준다. ② ie로 끝나면 ie를 y로 고치고 ing를 붙여 준다. ③ [1개모음+1개자음]으로 끝나면 마지막 자음 하나를 더 써 주고 ing를 붙여 준다. ④ e로 끝나면 e를 없애고 ing를 붙인다. ⑤ [1개모음+1개자음]으로 끝나면, 마지막 자음 하나를 더 써 주고ing를 붙여 준다.

03 lie의 −ing형은 lying이다.

04 Is he~?로 질문하면 Yes, he is. 나 No, he isn't로 대답한다.

05 현재진행형의 부정문은 be동사 뒤에 not을 붙이면 된다.

06 ③에서 have는 '가지고 있다'의 의미가 아니라, '먹다'의 의미이므로 현재진행형이 가능하다.

07 yesterday, last night는 과거를 나타내는 부사이며 tomorrow, tomorrow morning은 미래를 나타내는 부사, now(지금)는 현재를 나타내는 부사이다.

08 I가 1인칭 단수이므로 현재형으로 고칠 때는 be동사를 없애고, 동사의 원형을 쓰면 된다.

09 She가 3인칭 단수이므로 현재형으로 고칠 때는 be동사를 없애고, 동사원형에 s나 es를 붙여 준다.

10 현재진행형은 '~하고 있다', 현재형은 '~하다'로 해석된다.

 p.88

1 drives　2 is washing　3 catches
4 am enjoying　5 are crossing　6 are jogging
7 is repairing　8 is mixing　9 helps
10 are practicing

Review Test 1
p.90~97

Unit 1

01
1 are　2 is　3 is　4 are　5 is

02
1 There are two men
2 There isn't a mountain
3 There is some bread
4 There is little milk
5 There are a book and a pen

03
1 Is there a fish, there is
2 Are there ten boys, there aren't
3 There aren't a lot of taxis
4 Is there a lot of honey, there is
5 There aren't six cups
6 There isn't a lot of cheese
7 There isn't a girl
8 Are there three stories, there aren't
9 There aren't two cell phones
10 Is there a river, there isn't

Unit 2

01
1 studies　2 likes　3 know　4 goes　5 has
6 play　7 washes

02
1 He　2 She　3 You　4 Dad　5 Tom and Jane
6 Uncle　7 I

03
1 takes　2 plays　3 do　4 drinks　5 cries
6 goes　7 has　8 catch　9 enjoys　10 carries
11 tastes　12 fixes　13 fly　14 speak　15 hopes

Unit 3

01
1 doesn't, know　2 doesn't, have　3 don't, eat
4 don't, play　5 doesn't, study

02
1 Does, speak　2 Do, write　3 Does, like
4 Do, live　5 Does, drive

03
1 too　2 too　3 either

04
1 Does he sleep, he does
2 Do they go, they do
3 Susan doesn't like
4 I don't have
5 Does she keep, she doesn't
6 Tom doesn't know
7 Do you have, I don't

05

1 too   2 either   3 too

Unit 4

01

1 is, eating   2 am, coming   3 are, singing

4 is, driving   5 are, chatting

02

1 He is choosing   2 I am learning

3 Mom is doing   4 They are sailing

5 Tom is talking

03

1 He isn't taking

2 Is she cutting, she is

3 I'm not cooking

4 Are they playing ,they are

5 We aren't going

6 Is Tom teaching, he isn't

7 It isn't raining

8 Is it snowing, it isn't

9 The horses aren't running

10 Is your sister buying, she isn't

내/신/대/비 1   p.98~102

01 ④   02 ⑤   03 There is a bed in his room.

04 ④   05 There aren't a few trees in the park.

06 ②   07 They are → There are   08 ③   09 ①

10 ④   11 ③   12 ①   13 ⑤   14 ③   15 goes →

go   16 ②   17 ③   18 ③   19 ①   20 ②

21 Jane is playing the cello.   22 ③   23 ④

24 ①   25 jogs/ is jogging

05 형용사

기초다지기   p.108~111

1

1 한정적용법. 달콤한 / 서술적용법. 달콤하다.

2 서술적용법. 키가 크다 / 한정적용법. 키가 큰

3 서술적용법. 빠르다 / 한정적용법. 빠른

4 한정적용법. 긴 다리 / 서술적용법. 길다

5 서술적용법. 화창하다 / 한정적용법. 화창한

2   1 slow-fast   2 cold-hot   3 young-old

4 sad-glad   5 bright-dark   6 strong-weak

7 shallow-deep   8 tall-short   9 easy-difficult

10 hungry-full   11 wet-dry   12 healthy-sick, ill

13 low-high   14 light-heavy   15 happy-unhappy

3   1 small-big   2 diligent-lazy   3 short-long

4 kind-unkind   5 pretty-ugly   6 foolish-smart

7 full-empty   8 clean-dirty   9 expensive-cheap

10 rich-poor   11 busy-free   12 open-closed

13 dangerous-safe   14 fat-skinny   15 good-bad

4

1 look worse, look good, look happy

2 sounds sad, sounds cold, sound crazy

3 smells salty, smells sour, smells bad

4 tastes good, tastes sour, taste sweet

5 feel sleepy, feel cold, feel lonely

꼭꼭다지기   p.112~119

1

1 my, new, partner

2 a, very, long, new, coat

▶'관사+부사+형상.신.구+명사'의 어순에 유의한다.

3 very, small, insects

4 a, diligent, woman

5 a, very, deep, river

6 his, great, paintings
   ▶'소유격+형용사+명사'의 어순에 유의한다.

7 a, very, strong, young, man

8 two, big, brown, leaves
   ▶'수량+대.소+형상+명사'의 어순이다.

9 three, bad, thieves

10 a, very, sunny, day

2

1 his, red, tie

2 a, good, soccer player

3 five, short, red, skirts

4 a, very, heavy, watermelon

5 three, little, pretty, girls

6 high, new, buildings

7 a, poor, beggar

8 a, very, short, fat, farmer

9 our, good, friends

10 an, expensive, old, clock

3 1 추운. am, cold ▶'춥다'란 말은 우리말에서는 '추운+이다'의 순이지만, 영어에서는 '이다(am)+추운(cold)'이다. 2 더러운. are, dirty 3 이다. is, shallow 4 이다. is, dry 5 문을 닫은. is, closed 6 이다. is, stormy 7 아픈. is, sick 8 신선한. are, fresh 9 놀라운. is, wonderful 10 부유한. are, rich

4 1 is, low 2 is, lazy 3 are, yellow 4 is, big 5 are, difficult 6 is, empty 7 am, full 8 are, dangerous 9 is, muggy ▶It은 3인칭 단수이므로 is를 쓴다. 10 is, free

5 1 aren't, weak 2 isn't, unhappy 3 is, safe 4 aren't, cheap 5 is, lazy 6 aren't, dry 7 aren't, short 8 isn't, short 9 are, fast 10 is, closed

6 1 are, old 2 is, full 3 isn't, poor 4 is, deep 5 isn't, cold 6 are, high 7 are, heavy 8 isn't, sick (unhealthy) 9 is, bright 10 aren't, unwise

7 1 tastes bitter 2 smells hot 3 sounds interesting 4 looks pale 5 feel comfortable 6 tastes wonderful 7 looks warm 8 sounds strange 9 looks dead 10 smell awful

8 1 smell good 2 look nice 3 looks fantastic 4 tastes fishy 5 feel hungry 6 feels hard 7 looks cold 8 looks nervous 9 tastes sour 10 feel light

 p.120~121

1

1 unkind a girl → an unkind girl.

2 bigs → big. ▶big은 형용사이므로 s를 붙이지 않는다.

3 very a hungry → a very hungry

4 foolish → are foolish

5 blues → blue ▶blue는 형용사이므로 s를 붙이지 않는다.

6 old big → big old

7 an → a

8 large is → is large

9 slim very dancers → very slim dancers

10 new seven → seven new
   ▶이 때의 순서는 '수량+대.소+신.구+명사'이다.

11 greens → green ▶green은 형용사이므로 s를 붙이지 않는다.

12 merrily → merry

13 strongly → strong.

14 boys little → little boys

②

1 very exciting a game → a very exciting game

2 empty → are empty
  ▶ 비어있다는 '이다+비어있는'이므로 be동사 are가 빠지면 안된다.

3 comfortable very → very comfortable

4 wets → wet. ▶ wet은 형용사이므로 s를 붙이지 않는다.

5 lovely small → small lovely
  ▶ 이 때의 순서는 '소유격+대,소+형상+명사'이다.

6 sweetly → sweet.

7 very a hot stove → a very hot stove

8 deeply → deep

9 bigs → big

10 old rich → rich old
  ▶ 이 때의 순서는 '부사+형상+신,구+명사'이다.

11 terribly → terrible

12 kind very → very kind

13 happily → happy

14 bitterly → bitter

실전Test
p.122~125

> **01** ③   **02** ③   **03** ⑤   **04** ④   **05** a. rainy,
> b. cloudy,   c. windy,   d. snowy,   e. stormy,
> f. foggy,   g. muggy   **6** tall, fat   **7** My father is a
> very famous old doctor.   **8** un   **9** ⑤   **10** ④

01 fast ↔ slow, small ↔ big

02 '관사+부사+형용사+명사'의 순서

03 warm은 형용사이므로 s를 붙일 수 없다.

04 ① 소유격 뒤에는 단수명사가 오더라도 a를 붙이지 않는다. ② 수량 +형상+명사 ③ a+very+형용사+명사 ④ 수량+대,소+명사 ⑤ 소 유격+형용사+명사

05 명사 뒤에 y를 붙여 형용사를 만든 경우이다.

06 short와 반대의 의미를 가진 형용사는 tall이고, skinny와 반대의 의미를 가진 형용사는 fat이다.

07 a+very+형용사(형상+신,구)+명사

08 happy, kind, wise, able 등은 앞에 un을 붙여 반대의 의미를 갖는 형용사를 만든다.

09 happy, sad, lovely, sick는 형용사이며, cutely는 부사이다.

10 ①②③⑤는 형용사가 명사를 꾸며주는 한정적 용법으로 쓰였으며, ④는 주어를 보충 설명하는 보어로 쓰여, 서술적 용법으로 쓰였다.

p.126

1 is, poor   **2** smells, awful   **3** feel, better
4 three, little, lovely   **5** looks, nice   **6** three, difficult   **7** is, windy, foggy   **8** a, big, old
9 taste, sour   **10** interesting, new

06 some, any와 many, much, a lot of

기초 다지기   p.130~133

1 1 candies 2 trees 3 butter 4 rulers
5 sunflowers 6 cheese 7 any

1 some 2 any 3 some 4 any 5 some
6 any 7 some

2 1 much 2 many 3 much 4 many
5 many 6 many 7 many 8 many 9 much
10 many 11 much 12 many 13 many
14 many 15 much

3
1 many, a lot of   2 many, a lot of
3 many, a lot of
4 much, a lot of ▶의문문, 부정문에는 셀 수 없는 명사 앞에 much, a lot of 둘 다 사용 가능하다.
5 a lot of ▶긍정문에서 셀 수 없는 명사 앞에는 a lot of 가 온다.
6 a lot of ▶긍정문에서 셀 수 없는 명사 앞에는 a lot of 가 온다.
7 many ▶very, so, too뒤에는 a lot of 가 올수 없다.
8 many, a lot of
9 much ▶very, so, too뒤에는 a lot of 가 올수 없다.
10 a lot of ▶긍정문에서 셀 수 없는 명사 앞에는 a lot of 가 온다.
11 many, a lot of   12 many, a lot of
13 many, a lot of
14 a lot of ▶긍정문에서 셀 수 없는 명사 앞에는 a lot of 가 온다.
15 many, a lot of

4
1 a lot of ▶긍정문에서 셀 수 없는 명사 앞에는 a lot of 가 온다.
2 a lot of ▶긍정문에서 셀 수 없는 명사 앞에는 a lot of 가 온다.
3 many, a lot of
4 a lot of ▶긍정문에서 셀 수 없는 명사 앞에는 a lot of 가 온다.
5 many, a lot of
6 a lot of ▶긍정문에서 셀 수 없는 명사 앞에는 a lot of 가 온다.

7 much ▶very, so, too뒤에는 a lot of 가 올수 없다.
8 many, a lot of
9 much, a lot of ▶의문문, 부정문에는 셀 수 없는 명사 앞에 much, a lot of 둘 다 사용 가능하다.
10 much ▶very, so, too뒤에는 a lot of 가 올수 없다.
11 many, a lot of   12 many, a lot of
13 a lot of ▶긍정문에서 셀 수 없는 명사 앞에는 a lot of 가 온다.
14 much, a lot of ▶의문문, 부정문에는 셀 수 없는 명사 앞에 much, a lot of 둘 다 사용 가능하다.
15 a lot of ▶긍정문에서 셀 수 없는 명사 앞에는 a lot of 가 온다.

꼭꼭 다지기   p.134~137

1 1 any 2 any 3 some 4 any 5 any
6 any 7 some 8 any 9 any 10 some
11 any 12 any 13 some 14 any 15 some

2
1 Does Mr. Kim keep any pigs?
2 She doesn't wash any strawberries.
3 I don't write any novels.
4 Does her mother help any poor people?
5 Does he teach any smart students?
6 She doesn't slice any cheese off.
7 Do you visit any places in Turkey?
8 There aren't any holidays in this month.
9 Do you need any help now?
10 It doesn't have any dangers.

3
1 many, a lot of
2 much, a lot of ▶의문문, 부정문에는 셀 수 없는 명사 앞에 much, a lot of 둘다 사용 가능하다.
3 many, a lot of
4 much, a lot of ▶vegetable은 셀 수 없는 명사이다.
5 Many, A lot of   6 many, a lot of
7 many
8 a lot of ▶긍정문에는 셀 수 없는 명사 앞에 a lot of 가 온다.
9 many, a lot of   10 a lot of

11 much | 12 much, a lot of

13 a lot of | 14 many, a lot of

15 much, a lot of ▶yogurt는 셀 수 없는 명사이며 의문문, 부정문에는 셀 수 없는 명사 앞에 much, a lot of 둘 다 사용 가능하다.

4

1 much, a lot of | 2 many, a lot of

3 many, a lot of | 4 a lot of

5 much, a lot of | 6 many, a lot of

7 much ▶very, so, too뒤에는 a lot of 가 올수 없다.

8 much | 9 a lot of

10 many, a lot of | 11 many, a lot of

12 many | 13 a lot of

14 many, a lot of | 15 many

실력 다지기
p.138~139

1 1 student → students 2 some → any

3 some → any 4 any → some 5 some → any

6 sugars → sugar 7 any → some 8 sample →

samples 9 some → any 10 bridge → bridges

11 some → any 12 any → some ▶권유의 의미를 가진 의문문이므로 some을 사용한다. 13 any → some

14 some → any 15 word → words

2

1 many → a lot of, much

2 ball → balls 3 many → a lot of

▶긍정문에는 셀 수 없는 명사 앞에 a lot of 가 온다.

4 much → many/a lot of

5 Much → A lot of

▶긍정문에는 셀 수 없는 명사 앞에 a lot of 가 온다.

6 time → times 7 funs → fun

8 child → children 9 many → much/a lot of

10 much → many, a lot of

11 much → many, a lot of

12 many → much, a lot of

13 tiger → tigers 14 Much → A lot of

15 leaf → leaves

01 ③ 02 ② 03 ⑤ 04 ① 05 Much →
Many, A lot of 06 ③ 07 a lot of 08 ③,⑤
09 a lot of → much 10 ③

01 셀 수 없는 명사는 복수를 만들 수 없다.

02 부정문, 의문문에는 some 대신 any를 쓴다.

04 권유문은 some을 쓰고, 부정문, 의문문에는 some 대신 any를 쓴다.

05 긍정문에는 셀 수 있는 명사 앞에 many, a lot of 가 온다.

06 권유, 부탁을 할 때는 some을 쓴다.

08 의문문, 부정문에는 셀 수 없는 명사 앞에 much, a lot of 둘다 사용 가능하다.

09 very, so, too뒤에는 a lot of 가 올수 없다.

10 명사의 종류, 문장의 종류와 관계없이 a lot of를 쓸 수 있다.

Quiz!
p.144

1 some 2 any 3 some 4 some 5 any

6 some 7 any

1 Many, A lot of 2 many, a lot of 3 many, a lot of 4 much, a lot of 5 a lot of 6 much

7 many, a lot of

07 부사

p.148~153

1 1 fast 2 safe 3 late 4 easily
5 dangerous 6 high 7 quickly 8 heavy
9 loud/ loudly 10 hard 11 slow/slowly
12 good 13 carefully 14 angrily 15 beautiful

2 1 sometimes 2 hardly 3 결코 ~않다
4 always 5 often 6 never 7 sometimes
8 드물게, 좀처럼 ~않다 9 usually 10 항상 11 보통
12 rarely/seldom 13 자주, 종종 14 거의 ~않다

3
1 flies / 부사, 높게(이) 날아간다. building / 형용사, 높은 빌딩이다.
2 works / 부사, 열심히 일한다. time / 형용사, 힘든 시간을 가진다.
3 leaves / 부사, 일찍 떠난다. winter / 형용사, 이른 겨울에 만난다.
4 dinner / 형용사, 늦은 저녁을 먹는다. stays up / 부사, 늦게까지 안 잔다.
5 is / 형용사, 빠르고 쉽다. is sinking / 부사, 빠르게 가라앉고 있다.

4 1 fast 2 well 3 happily 4 easily
5 perfect 6 kind 7 angry 8 perfectly
9 slow/slowly 10 good 11 easily 12 early
13 bad ▶be bad(poor) at ~을 잘 못하다. 14 dangerous
15 quickly

5 1 early 2 heavy 3 loud 4 late
5 easy ▶형용사의 서술적 용법이다. 6 very 7 safely
8 angrily 9 carefully 10 well 11 dangerous
▶형용사의 서술적 용법이다. 12 kindly 13 perfectly
14 good 15 high

6 1 ② 2 ① 3 ② 4 ② 5 ② ▶will은 조동사이고
go는 일반동사이므로 always는 will과 go사이에 온다. 6 ①
7 ② 8 ① 9 ① 10 ② 11 ② 12 ① 13 ①
14 ② 15 ②

p.154~157

1 1 beautifully 2 easily 3 careful 4 nice
5 dangerously 6 safe ▶형용사의 서술적 용법이다.
7 perfectly 8 softly 9 hard ▶hard는 형용사의 서술적
용법으로 쓰였으며, hard는 형용사와 부사의 형태가 같다. 10 high
▶high는 형용사, 부사가 같다. 11 loud ▶형용사의 서술적 용법이
다. 12 fast ▶fast는 형용사, 부사의 형태가 같다. 13 quietly
14 well ▶good의 부사형은 well이다. 15 good ▶형용사의 한
정적 용법이다.

2 1 slow, slowly, nicely 2 hard 3 quick ▶형
용사의 서술적 용법이다. 4 badly 5 difficult 6 safely
7 perfect ▶형용사의 서술적 용법이다. 8 carefully
9 Fast 10 late 11 nicely 12 heavily 13 early,
late ▶early, late 모두 형용사와 부사의 형태가 같다. 14 angry,
late ▶형용사의 서술적 용법이다. 15 hard

3 1 always drink 2 sometimes misses
3 is usually 4 often change 5 hardly reads
6 usually uses 7 rarely see 8 sometimes enjoy
9 is never 10 seldom plays

4
1 Jane seldom feeds her bird.
2 I never tide up my room.
3 He never tells a lie
4 We hardly play a computer game.

1 d, e, f, h, i, j
▶rarely, seldom, hardly, never는 부정문에 사용할 수 없다.

p.158~159

1 1 goes often → often goes 2 sad → sadly
3 lately → late 4 kindly explains → explains
kindly 5 often is → is often 6 honestly →
honest 7 quick → quickly ▶runs를 수식하는 부사의 형태
가 와야 하므로 quick(형용사)을 사용할 수 없다.

8 seldom doesn't → seldom ▶rarely, seldom, hardly, never는 부정문에 사용할 수 없다. 9 always can → can always 10 wakes sometimes → sometimes wakes 11 highly → high 12 doesn't 삭제 ▶rarely, seldom, hardly, never는 부정문에 사용할 수 없다. 13 doesn't 삭제 14 hardly → hard ▶hard는 형용사와 부사의 형태가 같다. 15 sometimes are → are sometimes

2 1 never 삭제 2 often is → is often 3 real → really 4 fastly → fast 5 works never → never works 6 good → well 7 easy → easily 8 practices always → always practices 9 usually is → is usually 10 cutely → cute 11 easy → easily 12 rarely 삭제 13 earlily → early 14 new → newly 15 deeply → deep

실전Test
p.160~163

01 ③ 02 ④ 03 ⑤ 04 ② 05 ③ 06 ②
07 ③ 08 ① 09 ⑤ 10 beautifully, well

01 good의 부사 형태는 well이다.

02 early는 형용사와 부사의 형태가 같다.

03 ①②③④는 부사, ⑤는 '늦은'이라는 의미의 형용사이다.

04 빈도부사는 일반동사 앞에 위치한다.

05 빈도부사는 be동사 뒤에 위치한다.

06 Lisa가 7시에 일어나는 횟수가 80% 이상 이므로 usually에 해당된다.

07 always는 100%를 나타내는데, Lisa는 일요일에만 7시에 일어나지 않는다.

08 보어자리이므로 형용사만 올 수 있고, 부사는 올 수 없다.

09 ①②③④는 형용사와 부사가 같은 형태이다.

10 beautiful은 ly를 붙여 부사를 만들지만 good의 부사는 완전히 형태가 다른 well이다.

 p.164

1 slow 2 easily 3 carefully 4 fast
5 dangerous 6 nicely

1 always 2 never 3 sometimes

1 ① 2 ① 3 ② 4 ①

08 비교

p.168~171

기초다지기

1

1 taller - tallest
2 better - best
3 happier - happiest
4 stronger - strongest
5 faster - fastest
6 more foolish - most foolish
7 better - best
8 wiser - wisest
9 hotter - hottest
10 easier - easiest
11 more famous - most famous
12 more - most
13 more useful - most useful
14 younger - youngest
15 worse - worst

2

1 warmer - warmest
2 cleverer - cleverest
3 busier - busiest
4 more beautiful - most beautiful
5 smaller - smallest
6 nicer - nicest
7 more expensive - most expensive
8 more interesting - most interesting
9 bigger - biggest
10 worse - worst
11 lighter - lightest
12 prettier - prettiest
13 more important - most important
14 more - most
15 quicker - quickest

3

1 faster   2 the biggest   3 larger
4 more beautiful   5 the busiest   6 strong
7 interesting   8 better   9 easy   10 worse
11 in   12 the hottest   13 in   14 of   15 worse

4

1 hotter   2 more useful   3 slow   4 new
5 in   6 the fastest   7 louder   8 in   9 more
expensive   10 of   11 quick   12 of   13 more
boring   14 harder   15 more dangerous

p.172~175

꼭꼭다지기

1

1 as young as
2 bigger than
3 as difficult as
4 brighter than
5 heavier than
6 the most important   ▶최상급+of+복수(명사)
7 faster than
8 the bravest of   ▶최상급+of+복수(명사)
9 sweeter than
10 the most intelligent in   ▶최상급+in+범위

2

1 warmer than
2 as bitter as
3 softer than
4 worse than
5 the best teacher
6 the most colorful of
7 the most lovely doll
8 lighter than
9 as wise as
10 faster than

3

1 the easiest
2 freer than
3 more famous
4 more difficult than
5 as nice as
6 older than
7 as cold as
8 as well as
9 easier than
10 the most beautiful

4

1 better than
2 as interesting as
3 the best month
4 more useful than
5 the worst   ▶나쁜'bad'의 비교급-최상급은 worse-worst이다.
6 better than
7 worse than
8 as dark as
9 as pretty as
10 the richest in

1 1 heaviest → heavier 2 the clever → the cleverest 3 of → than 4 taller → tall 5 dark → darker 6 famousest → most famous ▶3음절 이상의 비교급, 최상급은 more, most를 붙여 만든다. more expensive – most expensive. 7 as 삭제 8 usefuler → more useful 9 friendlier → more friendly ▶ful, able, less, ous, ive, ish, ly등으로 끝나는 2음절어의 비교급, 최상급은 more, most를 붙여 만든다. 10 of → in 11 more dangerous → dangerous 12 of → in 13 younger → the youngest 14 your → you 15 bader → worse

2 1 he than → than he 2 good → better 3 in → of 4 faster → fastest 5 in → of 6 most → more 7 more warm → warmer 8 big → bigger 9 greater → greatest 10 in → of 11 best → good 12 expensivier → more expensive ▶3음절 이상의 비교급, 최상급은 more, most를 붙여 만든다. 13 busier → busiest 14 low → lower 15 happier → happiest

실전Test

01 ④ 02 as, as, than, than 03 ③ 04 Math is as easy as English. 05 Woojin 06 Mina 07 ② 08 Seoul is the largest city in Korea 09 ④ 10 ③

01 good－better－best

02 fat가 원급이므로 as~as가 와야하고 happier는 happy의 비교급이므로 뒤에 than이 와야 하고, sweeter는 sweet의 비교급이므로 뒤에 than 이 와야 한다.

03 3음절 이상의 형용사나 부사는 앞에 more를 붙여 비교급을 만든다.

04 원급 비교는 'as+형용사/부사+as'를 이용한다.

05 우진이는 51kg으로 넷 중에 가장 무겁다.

06 미나와 강민이는 몸무게가 같으므로 원급 비교이다.

07 뒤에 than이 나온 것으로 보아 빈칸에는 비교급 표현이 와야 한다.

08 형용사의 최상급 앞에는 정관사 the를 붙여 주어야 한다.

09 of+복수명사, in+범위

10 빠르기를 비교하면 수진>동수>민호 순이다.

1 the highest 2 difficult 3 busier 4 the hottest 5 better 6 larger 7 big 8 richer 9 the cleverest 10 hard 11 faster 12 the most colorful 13 taller 14 young 15 the nicest

Review Test 2

Unit 5

01
1 warm water 2 sick child 3 sad movie 4 easy work 5 rainy day

02
1 a very difficult problem 2 my younger sister 3 a tall good boy ▶형용사의 순서는 '대/소+형상 + 명사' 4 small pretty dolls 5 a big old house ▶형용사의 순서는 '대/소+신/구 + 명사'

03
1 is wise 2 is difficult 3 are healthy 4 am hungry 5 is cold

04
1 looks old 2 tastes salty 3 smell sweet 4 sounds good 5 feel thirsty

Unit 6

01
1 some apples 2 some money 3 any dogs 4 any coins 5 any meat 6 some friends 7 any leftovers

02
1 many, a lot of 2 a lot of 3 much, a lot of

4 a lot of 5 many, a lot of 6 many, a lot of
7 a lot of

03
1 some butter 2 any skirts 3 any pens
4 some rice 5 any water 6 some oranges
7 some tea

04
1 many, a lot of books 2 a lot of sugar
3 Many, A lot of children 4 A lot of effort
5 many, a lot of stars 6 many, a lot of cars
7 a lot of help

Unit 7

01
1 dangerously 2 slow/slowly 3 beautifully
4 high 5 late 6 heavily 7 happily 8 early

02
1 ② 2 ① 3 ② 4 ② 5 ①

03
1 late 2 fast 3 safely 4 early 5 easily

04
1 is always 2 sometimes watch 3 usually goes
4 hardly does 5 never eat

Unit 8

01
1 higher - highest 2 wiser - wisest 3 easier
- easiest 4 bigger - biggest 5 more foolish -
most foolish 6 more useful - most useful ▶ful,
able, less, ous, ive, ish, ly등으로 끝나는 2음절어의 비교급, 최상급
은 more, most를 붙여 만든다. 7 better - best 8 worse -
worst

02
1 taller 2 high 3 the wisest 4 big
5 the most famous 6 better

03
1 as small as   2 more expensive than
3 the strongest   4 faster than
5 as well as   6 the most interesting
7 prettier than   8 the hottest
9 as famous as   10 worse than

내/신/대/비 2   p.192~196

01 ④ 02 ③ 03 windy, foggy 04 ⑤ ▶①, ③, ④는
형용사의 한정적 용법. ②는 '감각동사+형용사', ⑤는 서술적 용법
05 ① 06 free, short, low, full 07 ③ 08 ⑤
09 The man drinks a lot of milk everyday. 10 ①
11 ③ 12 ② ▶①, ③, ④, ⑤는 부사를 수식하는 부사. ②는 형용
사를 수식하는 부사 13 ⑤ 14 A very fat man 15 ④
16 nicely → nice 17 ② ▶빈도부사는 일반동사 앞에 온다.
18 ② 19 ④, ⑤ 20 ④ 21 heavier, younger
22 as old as 23 ③ 24 ④ 25 ④

종합문제 1회   p.198~201

01 Five rabbits are 02 There isn't a clock on
the TV. 03 ② 04 ④, ⑤ 05 ④ 06 ②
07 ③ 08 ③ 09 ① 10 ⑤ 11 ② 12 ②
13 Does → Do 14 too/either 15 ① 16 ⑤
17 ① 18 ③ 19 ④ 20 drinking → are
drinking ▶현재진행형은 'be동사+~ing'이다.

종합문제 2회   p.202~205

01 easy / windy 02 ① 03 ③ 04 ⑤
05 full 06 ④ 07 ② 08 some 09 banana
→ bananas 10 ① 11 ② 12 a lot of 13 ⑤
14 much → many, a lot of 15 ① ▶긍정문에는 셀
수 없는 명사 앞에 a lot of 가 온다. 16 ⑤ 17 ④
18 early, hard 19 always 20 ③

MEMO

MEMO

MEMO

MEMO